THE
ROCK
OF OUR
REDEEMER

THE
ROCK
OF OUR
REDEEMER

FACING THE FUTURE WITH FAITH, HOPE, AND POWER

DAVID A. BEDNAR

DESERET
BOOK

SALT LAKE CITY, UTAH

Library of Congress Cataloging-in-Publication Data
(CIP data on file)
ISBN 978-1-63993-368-6

Printed in the United States of America
Publishers Printing, Salt Lake City, UT

10   9   8   7   6   5   4   3   2   1

CONTENTS

SECTION 2
By Study and Also by Faith—Ask, Seek, and Knock

SECTION 3
Gather Together in One All Things in Christ— Obtaining the Greatest Perspective of Truth

PREFACE

Feeling discouraged and overwhelmed can be all too easy as we encounter the opposition and challenges of the latter days, even though we, as members of the restored Church of Jesus Christ, know that we are blessed to live in a remarkable time in the history of the world. The visitation of the Father and the Son to young Joseph Smith, the ushering in of the dispensation of the fulness of times, the ongoing restoration of the Savior's gospel, the coming forth of the Book of Mormon, and the return of priesthood authority, keys, and sacred covenants and ordinances truly are a latter day "marvelous work and a wonder" (see Isaiah 29:14; 2 Nephi 25:17–18; Doctrine and Covenants 4:1).

Yet Lucifer, the enemy of all righteousness, works relentlessly to thwart the purposes of God and the progress of His kingdom on the earth. Satan rebelled against Heavenly Father's plan of happiness in our premortal existence and sought to destroy the agency of all humankind (see Abraham 3:24–28; Doctrine and Covenants 29:36–37; Moses 4:1–4). His only desire is to make the sons and daughters of God miserable, just as he himself is miserable (see 2 Nephi 2:18, 27).

The intensifying opposition to the work of God was foretold by President Brigham Young. He stated, "It was revealed to me in the commencement of this Church, that the Church would spread, prosper, grow and extend, and that in proportion to the spread of the Gospel among the nations of the earth, so would the power of Satan rise."[1]

WE CANNOT LIVE ON BORROWED LIGHT

Amid the whirlwinds of wickedness and trials of mortality, how can we remain firm in our commitment to be devoted disciples of the Savior, stay on the covenant path, and find peace, hope, and power to face adversity?

While the Prophet Joseph Smith was confined in Liberty Jail, Apostles Brigham Young and Heber C. Kimball oversaw the evacuation of the Saints from Missouri. Almost thirty years later, Heber C. Kimball, then a member of the First Presidency, reflecting on his role in this history, said, "Let me say to you, that many of you will see the time when you will have all the trouble, trial and persecution that you can stand, and plenty of opportunities to show that you are *true to God and His work*."[2]

President Kimball continued: "To meet the difficulties that are coming, it will be necessary for you to have a knowledge of the truth of this work *for yourselves.* The difficulties will be of such a character that the man or woman who does not possess this personal knowledge or witness will fall. If you have not got the testimony, live right and call upon the Lord and cease not [until] you [attain] it. . . . The time will come when no man nor woman will be able to endure on borrowed light. Each will have to be guided by the light within himself. . . . If you don't have it you will not stand; therefore seek for the testimony of Jesus and cleave to it, that when the trying time comes you may not stumble and fall."[3]

THE SPECIAL SEASON IN WHICH WE LIVE

Having a strong, personal conviction that Heavenly Father and Jesus Christ live and of Their promises helps us stand firm in times of opposition and prepares us for the great opportunities and blessings available in this special season of the world. The holy scriptures and prophetic pronouncements help us to learn about and more fully appreciate the distinctive days in which we live.

The Prophet Joseph Smith declared: "The building up of Zion is a cause that has interested the people of God in every age; it is a theme upon which prophets, priests and kings have dwelt with peculiar delight; they have looked forward with joyful anticipation to the day in which we live; and fired with heavenly and joyful anticipations they have sung and written and prophesied of this our day; but they died without the sight; . . . it is left for us to see, participate in and help to roll forward the Latter-day glory."[4]

On another occasion, the Prophet revealed that "the heavenly Priesthood will unite with the earthly, to bring about those great purposes; . . . a work that God and angels have contemplated with delight for generations past; that fired the souls of the ancient patriarchs and prophets; a work that is destined to bring about the destruction of the powers of darkness, the renovation of the earth, the glory of God, and the salvation of the human family."[5]

"A marvelous and wonderful thing is coming to pass," President Gordon B. Hinckley emphasized. "The Lord is fulfilling His promise that His gospel shall be as the stone cut out of the mountain without hands which would roll forth and fill the whole earth, as Daniel saw in vision (see Daniel 2:31–45; Doctrine and Covenants 65:2). A great miracle is taking place right before our eyes."[6]

And President Russell M. Nelson taught, "Our Savior and Redeemer, Jesus Christ, will perform some of His mightiest works between now and when He comes again. We will see miraculous indications that God the Father and His Son, Jesus Christ, preside over this Church in majesty and glory."[7]

The spiritual significance of the latter days has been the focus of prophetic attention for centuries. And the special season in which we live is now and will continue to be filled with stunning spiritual developments and happenings.

I believe the preceding prophetic pronouncements highlight four important truths.

1. We are blessed to live at a time when we can learn, live, love, and share the gospel of Jesus Christ.
2. God's holy work is rolling forth across the entire world—and will continue to do so with increasing righteousness and power in preparation for the Second Coming of Jesus Christ.
3. Opposition to the work of the Lord likewise will continue to increase.
4. None of us can survive spiritually on borrowed light. Individually we must establish the foundation of our lives on the rock of Jesus Christ to withstand and overcome the individual and collective opposition we surely will encounter.

THE DISPENSATION OF THE FULNESS OF TIMES

I believe our responses to the supernal invitations to come unto the Lord Jesus Christ and establish the foundation of our lives upon Him and His gospel determine our eternal destiny. As we strive to strengthen our covenant connection with the Father and the Son; increase in spiritual knowledge, testimony, and conversion; and gather gospel truths together in one, each of us can be joyfully engaged in the marvelous opportunities and responsibilities of the latter days. We also can be fortified and guided to prevail over the growing opposition of the adversary.

"For by doing these things the gates of hell shall not prevail against you; yea, and the Lord God will disperse the powers of darkness from before you, and cause the heavens to shake for your good, and his name's glory" (Doctrine and Covenants 21:6).

BUILDING UPON THE ROCK OF OUR REDEEMER

Jesus Christ is our Redeemer (see Mosiah 15:6–9), our Mediator (see 2 Nephi 2:27–28), our Advocate with the Eternal Father (see Moroni 7:28), and the rock upon which we should build the foundation of our lives.

"Remember, remember that it is upon the rock of our Redeemer, who is Christ, the Son of God, that ye must build your foundation; that when the devil shall send forth his mighty winds, yea, his shafts in the whirlwind, yea, when all his hail and his mighty storm shall beat upon you, it shall have no power over you to drag you down to the gulf of misery and endless wo, because of the rock upon which ye are built, which is a sure foundation, a foundation whereon if men build they cannot fall" (Helaman 5:12).

If we are to share the gospel of Jesus Christ, prepare for His Second Coming, and remain steadfast and immovable amid the opposition in the latter days, we must strive to become solid, resolute, and firmly secured. To become steadfast disciples capable of enduring valiantly to the end (see Doctrine and Covenants 121:29), we must be connected to the rock of Jesus Christ.

ANCHORING OUR FOUNDATION TO THE ROCK OF JESUS CHRIST

The symbolism of Jesus Christ as the "rock" is most instructive. Please note that the Savior is not the foundation. Rather, we are admonished to build our spiritual foundation *upon Him.* President Russell M. Nelson taught, "Just as buildings and institutions have foundations, so do we as individuals have foundations that support our faith. Some are weak; some are strong. We can waffle 'like a wave of the sea driven with the wind and tossed' [James 1:6], or we can stand on a firm foundation and anchor ourselves with straps of spiritual steel, rooted and grounded to the timeless pillars of the gospel."[1]

A foundation is the part of a building that connects it to the ground. A strong foundation provides protection from natural disasters and many other destructive forces. A proper foundation also distributes the weight of a structure over a large area in order to avoid overloading the underlying soil and provides a level surface for construction.

A strong and reliable connection between the ground and a foundation is essential if a structure is to remain sturdy and stable over time. And for particular types of construction, anchor pins and steel rods can be used to attach the foundation of a building to bedrock, the hard, solid rock beneath surface materials such as soil and gravel.

In a similar way, the foundation of our lives must be securely connected to the rock of Jesus Christ if we are to remain firm and steadfast. The sacred covenants and ordinances of the Savior's restored gospel can be compared to the anchor pins and steel rods that are used to connect a building to the ground. Our spiritual anchors are secured ever more firmly and steadfastly to the "rock" of Christ every time we (1) faithfully receive, review, remember, and renew sacred covenants and the associated ordinances of the restored gospel and (2) ask, seek, and knock to learn for ourselves gospel doctrine and principles.

Now more than ever, we need to anchor our lives to the rock of Jesus Christ. "Wherefore, whoso believeth in God might with surety hope for a better world, yea, even a place at the right hand of God, which hope cometh of faith, maketh *an anchor* to the souls of men, which would make them sure and steadfast, always abounding in good works, being led to glorify God" (Ether 12:4; emphasis added).

Incrementally and increasingly, "in process of time" (Moses 7:21), "virtue [will] garnish [our] thoughts unceasingly," our "confidence [will wax stronger and stronger] in the presence of God," and "the Holy Ghost [will be our] constant companion" (Doctrine and Covenants 121:45–46). We will become more grounded, rooted, established, and settled (see Colossians 1:23; 2:7; 2 Peter 1:12).[2]

STEADFAST, IMMOVABLE, AND FIRM
FAITH IN JESUS CHRIST

The Lord Jesus Christ is the Only Begotten and Beloved Son of the Eternal Father, and He invites each of us to come unto and be perfected in Him (see Moroni 10:32–33; Matthew 5:48; 11:28–30). Responding to this invitation is the spiritual pursuit of a lifetime and the primary purpose of Heavenly Father's great plan of happiness for His children. "For behold, this is my work and my glory—to bring to pass the immortality and eternal life of man" (Moses 1:39).

The gospel truths discussed in this book can help us as we seek earnestly for the spiritual gift of faith in the Savior. True faith is always focused in and on the *Lord Jesus Christ*—in Him as the Divine and Only Begotten Son of the Eternal Father and on Him and the redemptive mission He fulfilled.

"For he hath answered the ends of the law, and he claimeth all those who have faith in him; and they who have faith in him will cleave unto every good thing; wherefore he advocateth the cause of the children of men" (Moroni 7:28).

We should exercise faith in Jesus Christ, trusting and placing our confidence in Him as our Savior and relying upon His merits, mercy, and grace (see 2 Nephi 2:8). As we do so, we are building our spiritual foundation on Jesus Christ, and we begin to become steadfast, immovable, and firm.

"Therefore, I would that ye should be *steadfast* and *immovable, always abounding in good works,* that Christ, the Lord God Omnipotent, may seal you his, that you may be brought to heaven, that ye may have everlasting salvation and eternal life, through the wisdom, and power, and justice, and mercy of him who created all things, in heaven and in earth, who is God above all" (Mosiah 5:15; emphasis added).

What does it mean to be steadfast and immovable? The word *steadfast* is used to suggest fixed in position, solid and firm, unshaken and resolute.[3] The word *immovable* is used to indicate that a person or thing is unalterable, firmly secured, and not subject to change. It also signifies the quality of being unyielding and incapable of being diverted from one's purpose.[4]

A building or structure that is firm and immovable must be built upon a strong foundation. President Russell M. Nelson, using the renovations of the Salt Lake Temple as an analogy, explained the strength that comes when our spiritual foundations are built on Jesus Christ: "The foundation of any building, particularly one as large as this one, must be strong and resilient enough to withstand earthquakes, corrosion, high winds, and the inevitable settling that affects all buildings. The complex task of strengthening now underway will reinforce this sacred temple with the foundation that can and will stand the test of time.

"We are sparing no effort to give this venerable temple, which had become increasingly *vulnerable*, a foundation that will withstand the forces of nature into the Millennium. In like manner, it is now time that we each implement extraordinary measures—perhaps measures we have never taken before—to strengthen our *personal spiritual* foundations. Unprecedented times call for unprecedented measures.

"My dear brothers and sisters, these *are* the latter days. If you and I are to withstand the forthcoming perils and pressures, it is imperative that we each have a *firm* spiritual foundation built upon the rock of our Redeemer, Jesus Christ."[5]

Also speaking of the Salt Lake Temple renovations, Elder Gary E. Stevenson taught, "The . . . seismic upgrade package for the temple [utilizes] base isolation technology. . . . This technology, recent in its development, begins at the very foundation of the temple, providing a robust defense against damage from an earthquake. In essence, it structurally strengthens the temple to stand steadfast, even as the earth and environment around it undergo an earthshaking seismic event.

". . . We might ask ourselves, 'How could this extensive renewal of the Salt Lake Temple inspire us to undergo our own spiritual *renewal, reconstruction, rebirth, revitalization, or restoration?*'

"An introspective look may reveal that we too and our families could benefit from our doing some needed maintenance and renovation work, even a seismic upgrade! We might start such a process by asking:

"'What does my foundation look like?'

"'What comprises the thick-walled, stable, strong cornerstones that are part of my personal foundation, upon which my testimony rests?'

"'What are the foundational elements of my spiritual and emotional character that will allow me and my family to remain steadfast and immovable, even to withstand the earthshaking and tumultuous seismic events that will surely take place in our lives?'

"These events, similar to an earthquake, are often difficult to predict and come in various levels of intensity—wrestling with questions or doubt, facing affliction or adversity, working through personal offenses with Church leaders, members, doctrine, or policy. The best defense against these lies in our spiritual foundation."[6]

The Book of Mormon prophet Samuel the Lamanite identifies in the following verses five fundamental elements for building our firm foundation upon the "rock" of the Lord Jesus Christ:

"And behold, ye do know of yourselves, for ye have witnessed it, that as many of them as are brought to the knowledge of the truth, and to know of the wicked and abominable traditions of their fathers, and are led to believe the holy scriptures, yea, the prophecies of the holy prophets, which are written, which leadeth them to faith on the Lord, and unto repentance, which faith and repentance bringeth a change of heart unto them—

"Therefore, as many as have come to this, ye know of yourselves are *firm* and steadfast in the faith, and in the thing wherewith they have been made free" (Helaman 15:7–8; emphasis added).

Please notice the specific steps outlined in these two verses. The first step is (1) belief in the teachings and prophecies of the holy prophets as recorded in the scriptures. Such belief (2) fosters faith in the Lord Jesus Christ. Faith in the Savior leads to (3) repentance. Faith in Christ and repentance bring about (4) the mighty change of heart. And as many as have diligently and faithfully followed these steps are (5) firm and steadfast in the faith. That is the Lord's blueprint for becoming steadfast and immovable.

Practical direction about becoming firm and steadfast also is provided by Mormon as he described the people in Helaman's day:

"Nevertheless they did fast and pray oft, and did wax stronger and stronger in their humility, and *firmer and firmer* in the faith of Christ, unto the filling their souls with joy and consolation, yea, even to the purifying and the sanctification of their hearts, which sanctification cometh because of their yielding their hearts unto God" (Helaman 3:35; emphasis added).

The Book of Mormon prophet Jacob highlighted in his

scriptural record the importance of becoming *firm* in our faith of Christ:

"But behold, I, Jacob, would speak unto you that are pure in heart. Look unto God *with firmness of mind*, and pray unto him with exceeding faith, and he will console you in your afflictions, and he will plead your cause, and send down justice upon those who seek your destruction.

"O all ye that are pure in heart, lift up your heads and receive the pleasing word of God, and feast upon his love; for ye may, *if your minds are firm*, forever" (Jacob 3:1–2; emphasis added).

A disciple's faith in the Lord Jesus Christ and firmness of mind, when complemented by an understanding heart, engenders a meek determination "to stand as [a witness] of God at all times and in all things, and in all places that ye may be in, even until death" (Mosiah 18:9). The firmness of mind described by Jacob is the spiritual remedy for "double-minded" men and women who alternate haphazardly between spiritual and worldly priorities and are unstable in all their ways.

In addition to providing a doctrinal explanation for how to develop lasting faith in Christ, the scriptures provide many noteworthy examples of individuals who are firm, steadfast, and immovable. Captain Moroni is one such striking example. He was strong and mighty, a man of perfect understanding. He did not delight in bloodshed but found joy in the liberty and freedom of his country and his people. Therefore, he labored exceedingly to secure their welfare and safety. His heart was full of thanksgiving to God for the privileges and blessings bestowed upon the Nephites (see Alma 48:11–12). Captain Moroni is described as "a man who was firm in the faith of Christ" (Alma 48:13).

The two thousand stripling warriors also can accurately be characterized as steadfast and immovable. They were all young men who were exceedingly valiant and courageous. They were also "men who were true at all times in whatsoever thing they were entrusted. Yea, they were men of truth and soberness" (Alma 53:20–21).

Many faithful disciples of the Savior in the Church today are blessed with spiritual strength and courage equal to or greater than that exemplified by Captain Moroni or the stripling warriors. They stand firm against the mocking and scorn of the world and live and defend principles of virtue, integrity, chastity, worthiness, and obedience.

These disciples are discerning brothers and sisters who look for and sit next to people who are alone in Church meetings and in a variety of other settings. They consistently strive to "comfort those that stand in need of comfort" (Mosiah 18:9) without expectations of acknowledgment or praise.

These disciples are spouses and children who support a companion, parent, or child who serves in a leadership position in the Lord's restored Church. Their steady, quiet, and typically unrecognized sustaining influence makes possible the blessing of many individuals and families in ways that will be fully known only in eternity.

These disciples are faithful married men and women who honor their covenant responsibility to multiply and replenish the earth. In an increasingly confused world beset with calamities and misplaced priorities, these courageous souls heed not the secular voices extolling self-centeredness; they reverence the sanctity and importance of life in Heavenly Father's plan of happiness for His children.

Many married couples also trust in God and rely on firm spiritual foundations when the righteous desires of their hearts are not realized how or when they had hoped and dreamed. They "wait upon the Lord" (Isaiah 40:31) and do not demand that He meet their mortal deadlines. "For since the beginning of the world have not men heard nor perceived by the ear, neither hath any eye seen, O God, besides thee, how great things thou hast prepared for [them] that waiteth for thee" (Doctrine and Covenants 133:45).

These disciples are the thousands and thousands of nursery leaders and Primary teachers who love and instruct the children of the Church each Sabbath day.

These disciples are dedicated children tenderly caring for aged parents, a sleep-deprived mother comforting a frightened child while standing guard as a "lioness at the gate" of her home,[7] Church members who arrive early and stay late to set up and take down chairs, and inspired individuals who invite family, friends, and associates to "come and see, come and help, and come and stay."[8]

I mention only a few selected examples of covenant-keeping and devoted disciples of Jesus Christ who are striving to anchor the foundations of their lives to the Savior. Millions of additional examples of Latter-day Saints who offer their "whole souls" (Omni 1:26) unto God are found in Christ-centered homes and in Church units around the world. In Captain Moroni, in the stripling warriors, and in so many Latter-day Saints today, we find the characteristics of firmness, of resoluteness, and of an absolute focus upon a compelling and correct purpose.

PURPOSE OF THIS BOOK

The purpose of this book is to emphasize the importance of building the spiritual foundation of our lives upon the rock of our Redeemer—our Savior Jesus Christ—so we can fulfill our sacred responsibilities in the Lord's latter-day work and stand steadfast against the whirlwinds of opposition and challenges.

We have already briefly reviewed scriptural truths about receiving the spiritual gift of faith and of becoming firm, steadfast, and immovable. In harmony with those teachings, this book focuses on three divine invitations:

1. to rely on our covenant connection with Heavenly Father and Jesus Christ;

2. to ask, seek, and knock; and

3. to gather together in one all things in Christ.

These three interrelated invitations work together to help disciples (1) seek appropriately for the spiritual gift of faith in the Lord Jesus Christ and (2) establish a firm foundation built upon the rock of Jesus Christ.

The sacred covenants and ordinances of the Savior's restored gospel are the divinely appointed and primary means to accomplish these eternal and essential objectives. Our personal *covenant connection* with God and the Lord Jesus Christ is the channel through which we can be blessed with purpose, power, and strength beyond our own.

Our foundations are also made firm through the knowledge we can obtain by the power of the Holy Ghost as we follow the Lord's invitation to *ask, seek, and knock*. And as we strive to learn for ourselves foundational gospel truths and develop strong, individual testimonies, we will find the greatest perspective and blessings as we *gather together in one all things **in Christ***.

1. ARMED WITH RIGHTEOUSNESS AND POWER— OUR COVENANT CONNECTION

God has made covenants with His faithful children since the beginning of the world. For example, Abraham was a great prophet who desired righteousness and obeyed all of God's commandments—including the command to offer as a sacrifice his precious son, Isaac. Because of Abraham's steadfast obedience, God made a covenant with him and promised the glorious blessings of a great posterity and that the nations of the earth would be blessed through his "seed" (see Genesis 22:16–18).

All nations are blessed by Abraham's posterity because those of his "seed" have the responsibility to share the gospel of Jesus Christ and invite all to receive by proper priesthood authority the ordinances of salvation and exaltation (see Abraham 2:9–10). The Lord later renewed this covenant with Abraham's son Isaac and his grandson Jacob and today through us who live and serve in the latter-day dispensation of the fulness of times.

How do these promises and blessings relate to you and me? Either by literal lineage or adoption, we are rightful heirs to God's promises to Abraham. We are sons and daughters of God and Abraham's "seed."

Covenant promises and blessings would not be possible without our Savior, Jesus Christ. He invites us to look to Him, come unto Him, learn of Him, and bind ourselves to Him through the covenants and ordinances of His restored gospel (see Doctrine and Covenants 6:36; 19:23; 43:9; 3 Nephi 12:20; Moroni 10:32–33; Matthew 11:29).

Precisely because faithfully honoring sacred covenants binds us securely to the Savior, He becomes the ultimate source of spiritual direction and strength in our lives. The covenant connection we have with our Heavenly Father and His resurrected and living

Son is individual and personal. It is the supernal source of perspective, hope, peace, and enduring joy.

Covenants and ordinances can also arm us with righteousness and power—even "the power of God in great glory" (1 Nephi 14:14)—through which we receive the blessings of guidance and direction, the promise of deliverance and enabling strength, and the power to withstand the evil influences and mocking voices of the world in which we live.

Covenants fuse our spiritual foundations to the rock of our Redeemer. Likewise, our foundations are strengthened and made firm through the personal testimonies and enduring conversion with which we can be blessed as we respond to the Savior's invitation to ask, seek, and knock.

2. ASKING, SEEKING, AND KNOCKING—
LEARNING FOR OURSELVES

To build upon the rock of our Redeemer, we need the power that comes from both sacred covenants and knowledge—personal, abiding knowledge that is acquired through the lifelong work of learning for ourselves.

One of the Savior's greatest invitations is found in His Sermon on the Mount: "Ask, and it shall be given you; seek, and ye shall find; knock, and it shall be opened unto you" (Matthew 7:7; see also 3 Nephi 14:7; Doctrine and Covenants 4:7). I believe the Lord's threefold exhortation is essential for the spiritual growth and well-being of each one of us in the commotion and contention of the latter days.

Reason is important and useful; however, it is neither the best nor the only way of knowing. A witness of truth by the power of the Holy Ghost that we invite into our soul produces a spiritual knowledge, an illumination, and a conviction more sure, more powerful, and more enduring than can be received through seeing, hearing, touching, or rational argument alone.

Asking, seeking, and knocking are how we become anxiously engaged in the process of acquiring this spiritual knowledge—of learning and understanding the fundamental doctrine and principles of the Savior's restored gospel. This pattern enables us to find answers to the questions, issues, and challenges that we may encounter in our daily lives.

If all we know about the gospel of Jesus Christ is what others have told us, then we will never know enough. If all we know is what we have read in commentaries written by others, then we will never know enough. Each of us must ask and seek and ask again. It is not a matter of having one question and learning one answer. Each answer and insight we receive will lead us to more questions in an ever-expanding pattern of obtaining knowledge line upon line. Asking and seeking constitute a vital part of the individual price we must pay to learn for ourselves.

I invite you to accept Alma's invitation to "awake and arouse your faculties" and to "exercise a particle of faith." Though you cannot see or touch it, does the "word" of truth "begin to swell within your breasts," and do these restored truths "enlarge [your] soul"? Can you feel by the power of the Holy Ghost the truth of these doctrinal foundations which cannot be touched or seen, but which begin to "enlighten [your] understanding" and "increase your faith" (Alma 32:27–29)?

3. GATHER TOGETHER IN ONE ALL THINGS IN CHRIST— OBTAINING THE GREATEST PERSPECTIVE OF TRUTH

Our search for spiritual knowledge and our faithful obedience are powerful means through which we establish firm, personal testimonies of gospel truths. And our efforts to ask, seek, and knock will lead to even greater perspective and blessings—and to a stronger foundation anchored to Jesus Christ—as we follow Paul's counsel to "gather together in one all things in Christ, both which are in heaven, and which are on earth; even in him" (Ephesians 1:10). Importantly, this vital gathering of truth is centered in and focused upon the Lord Jesus Christ because He is "the way, the truth, and the life" (John 14:6).

The invitation to gather together all things in Christ underscores the power of the Savior's gospel to transform and bless us that comes from discerning and applying the interrelatedness of its doctrine, principles, and practices. Only as we gather together in one all things in Christ, with firm focus upon Him, can gospel truths synergistically enable us to become what God desires us to become (see Matthew 5:48; 3 Nephi 12:48) and to endure valiantly to the end (see Doctrine and Covenants 121:29).

An analogy that helps illustrate this principle is that of a rope. A rope is an essential tool with which all of us are familiar. Ropes are made from strands of fabric, plants, wire, or other materials that are individually twisted or braided together. Interestingly, substances that may be quite unexceptional can be woven together and become exceptionally strong. Thus, effectively connecting and binding ordinary materials can produce an extraordinary tool.

In section 3, I present several doctrinal examples of how gathering "together in one all things in Christ" can strengthen our faith. "Gathering" doctrine and principles helps us develop a more comprehensive understanding of gospel truths, which is essential to ensuring our foundation is steadfast and immovable.

The Savior's gospel is a magnificent tapestry of truth "fitly framed" (Ephesians 2:21) and woven together. Just as a rope obtains its strength from many intertwined individual strands, as we learn and link together revealed gospel truths, we are blessed to receive the greatest perspective of truth and the richest blessings. We are blessed with an increased spiritual capacity through eyes that can see the Lord's influence in our lives and ears that can hear His voice (see Doctrine and Covenants 18:33–36; 136:32).

If you and I desire to become steadfast disciples of the Master, we need to establish our spiritual foundation appropriately and effectively upon Him. As we strengthen our covenant connection with the Redeemer, accept the invitations to learn gospel truths for ourselves, and gather together in one all things in Christ, we can be blessed with increased faith and develop a greater capacity to recognize Him as the "rock of our Redeemer" (Helaman 5:12). We become ever more anchored to Him—steadfast, firm, and immovable—able to withstand the challenges of our lives and empowered to participate more fully in the Lord's marvelous latter-day work.

ARMED WITH RIGHTEOUSNESS AND THE POWER OF GOD– OUR COVENANT CONNECTION

CHAPTER 1

BOUND TO THE SAVIOR THROUGH COVENANTS

Faithfully honoring sacred covenants yokes us securely to the Savior. As we bind ourselves to Him by worthily receiving and honoring covenants, the enabling blessings of His Atonement can become a reality in our lives.

The Savior said: "Come unto me, all ye that labour and are heavy laden, and I will give you rest.

"Take my yoke upon you, and learn of me; for I am meek and lowly in heart: and ye shall find rest unto your souls.

"For my yoke is easy, and my burden is light" (Matthew 11:28–30).

A yoke is a wooden beam, normally used between a pair of oxen or other animals, that allows them to pull together on a load. A yoke places animals side-by-side so they can move in unison to complete a task.

As disciples of Jesus Christ, we begin to take His yoke upon us as we accept sacred covenants and ordinances. A covenant is an agreement between God and His sons and daughters on the earth. God establishes the conditions of the covenant, and His children exercise their moral agency to learn about and consent to what He asks them to do. God then promises His sons and daughters certain blessings for their obedience.[1]

Ordinances are sacred acts, performed by the authority of the holy priesthood, that have spiritual purpose, have eternal significance, and are related to God's laws and statutes.[2] Ordinances also teach us about the nature of the covenants we agree to and accept in our lives.

In President Russell M. Nelson's first message as President of The Church of Jesus Christ of Latter-day Saints, he emphasized the importance of gospel covenants. He said:

"To each member of the Church I say, keep on the covenant path. Your commitment to follow the Savior by making covenants with Him and then keeping those covenants will open the door to every spiritual blessing and privilege available to men, women, and children everywhere."[3]

The Lord Jesus Christ invites each of us to "partake of his salvation, and the power of his redemption" (Omni 1:26). The promises, blessings, and power of the sacred covenants we make with Him can change our hearts, provide spiritual direction and protection, and enable us to have enduring joy.

Many of us already made our initial, or our first, covenants when we were baptized, were confirmed as members of The Church of Jesus Christ of Latter-day Saints, and received the gift of the Holy Ghost. And as we progress in the restored gospel, we have or will make more covenants. The most sacred covenants are received only in a holy temple—the house of the Lord.

Elder Dale G. Renlund taught, "The term *covenant path* refers to a series of covenants whereby we come to Christ and connect to Him. Through this covenant bond, we have access to His eternal power. The path begins with faith in Jesus Christ and repentance, followed by baptism and receiving the Holy Ghost. Jesus Christ showed us how to enter the path when He was baptized. According to the New Testament Gospel accounts in Mark and Luke, Heavenly Father spoke directly to Jesus at His baptism, saying, 'Thou art my beloved Son; in thee I am well pleased' [Luke 3:22; see also Mark 1:11]. When we embark on the covenant path through baptism, I can imagine Heavenly Father saying a similar thing to each of us: 'Thou art my dear child in whom I delight. Keep going.'"[4]

You and I are "the children of the covenant" (3 Nephi 20:26). To the people in the land of Bountiful, the Savior emphasized the eternal importance of the ordinance of baptism (see 3 Nephi 11:19–39) and receiving the Holy Ghost (see 3 Nephi 11:35–36; 12:6; 18:36–38). In a similar manner, you and I are admonished to turn toward and learn from Christ and to come unto Him through the covenants and ordinances of His restored gospel. As we do so, we will eventually and ultimately come to know Him (see John 17:3), "in his own time, and in his own way, and according to his own will" (Doctrine and Covenants 88:68).

A PERSONAL CONNECTION THROUGH COVENANTS

The covenants into which we enter are individual and personal. They are administered one by one. Being yoked with and bound to the Lord Jesus Christ and Heavenly Father (see Matthew 11:28–30) through sacred covenants and ordinances simply means that we trust in the Savior as our Advocate and Mediator and rely on His merits, mercy, and grace during the journey of life (see Moroni 7:28; Doctrine and Covenants 110:4; John 14:6; 1 Timothy 2:5; Doctrine and Covenants 107:19; 2 Nephi 2:8). It means we can receive the cleansing, healing, and strengthening blessings of His infinite and eternal Atonement (see Alma 7:11–13).

Living and loving covenant commitments create a connection with the Lord that is deeply personal and spiritually powerful. As we honor the conditions of sacred covenants and ordinances, we gradually and incrementally are drawn closer to Him (see 3 Nephi 27:14–15) and experience the impact of His divinity and living reality in our lives. Jesus then becomes much more than the central character in scripture stories; His example and teachings influence our every desire, thought, and action.

"Once we make a covenant with God," said President

Russell M. Nelson, "we leave neutral ground forever. God will not abandon His relationship with those who have forged such a bond with Him. In fact, all those who have made a covenant with God have access to a special kind of love and mercy. In the Hebrew language, that covenantal love is called *hesed* (חֶסֶד). . . .

"*Hesed* is a unique term describing a covenant relationship in which both parties are bound to be loyal and faithful to each other. . . .

"Once you and I have made a covenant with God, our relationship with Him becomes much closer than before our covenant. Now we are bound together. Because of our covenant with God, He will never tire in His efforts to help us, and we will never exhaust His merciful patience with us. Each of us has a special place in God's heart."[5]

THOU SHALT ABIDE IN ME

As we exercise our moral agency to take upon ourselves His yoke (see Matthew 11:29–30) through the covenants and ordinances of the restored gospel, we begin to abide in the Lord. The Lord Jesus Christ extends to each of us the invitation to abide in Him (John 15:4–9).

The word *abide* denotes remaining fixed or stable and enduring without yielding. President Jeffrey R. Holland explained that "abiding" as an action means "'[to] stay—but [to] stay *forever.*' That is the call of the gospel message to . . . everyone . . . in the world. Come, but come to remain. Come with conviction and endurance. Come permanently, for your sake and the sake of all the generations who must follow you."[6] Thus, we abide in Christ as we are firm and steadfast in our devotion to the Redeemer and His holy purposes, in times both good and bad (see John 15:10).

Of temple ordinances and covenants, President Nelson taught, "The temple lies at the center of strengthening our faith and spiritual fortitude because the Savior and His doctrine are the very heart of the temple. Everything taught in the temple, through instruction and through the Spirit, increases our understanding of Jesus Christ. His essential ordinances bind us to Him through sacred priesthood covenants. Then, as we keep our covenants, He endows us with *His* healing, strengthening power [see Doctrine and Covenants 109:15, 22]. And oh, how we will need His power in the days ahead.

"We have been promised that 'if [we] are prepared [we] shall not fear' [Doctrine and Covenants 38:30; see also Doctrine and Covenants 10:55]. This assurance has profound implications today. The Lord has declared that despite today's unprecedented challenges, those who build their foundations upon Jesus Christ, and have learned how to draw upon His power, need not succumb to the unique anxieties of this era."[7]

We abide in Him by striving continually to strengthen our individual covenant bond with the Father and the Son. For example, praying sincerely to the Eternal Father in the name of His Beloved Son deepens and fortifies our covenant connection with Them.

We abide in Him by truly feasting upon the words of Christ. The Savior's doctrine draws us, as children of the covenant, closer to Him (see 3 Nephi 27:14–15) and will tell us all things what we should do (see 2 Nephi 32:3).

We abide in Him by preparing earnestly to participate in the ordinance of the sacrament, reviewing and reflecting on our covenant promises and repenting sincerely. Worthily partaking of the sacrament is a witness to God that we are willing to take upon ourselves the name of Jesus Christ and strive to "always remember him" (Moroni 4:3; 5:2).

And we abide in Him by serving God as we serve His children and minister to our brothers and sisters (see Mosiah 2:17).

The Savior said, "If ye keep my commandments, ye shall abide in my love; even as I have kept my Father's commandments, and abide in His love" (John 15:10).

We build our lives upon the rock of Jesus Christ and His Atonement through the covenants and ordinances of His gospel. We are connected securely to and with Heavenly Father and the Savior as we worthily receive and faithfully remember and honor those holy commitments. As we do our best to live in accordance with the obligations we have accepted, that bond is the source of spiritual strength and stability in all of the seasons of our lives.

CHAPTER 2

THE BLESSINGS OF
DIRECTION AND STRENGTH

———————

Our covenant bond with Heavenly Father and the Savior is the source of spiritual direction and strength. I intentionally use the words *direction* and *strength* to describe the blessings that flow from fidelity to gospel covenants and ordinances. Let me briefly explain why I believe those two words are so important for us to understand.

COVENANTS, ORDINANCES, AND DIRECTION

President Russell M. Nelson has taught us that "the joy we feel has little to do with the circumstances of our lives and everything to do with the focus of our lives.

"When the focus of our lives is on God's plan of salvation . . . and Jesus Christ and His gospel, we can feel joy regardless of what is happening—or not happening—in our lives. Joy comes from and because of Him. He is the source of all joy."[1]

Please note how President Nelson used the phrase "the focus of our lives" two times. I invite you to consider how covenants are the primary source of the essential focus he describes.

Sacred covenants and ordinances operate in our lives much like a compass. A compass is a device used to indicate the cardinal directions of north, south, east, and west for purposes of navigation and geographic orientation. In a similar way, our covenants and ordinances point us to and help us always remember the Lord Jesus Christ as we press forward on the covenant path.

Recall that the Liahona described in the Book of Mormon was prepared by the Lord and given to Lehi and his family after they left Jerusalem and were traveling in the wilderness (see Alma 37:38; Doctrine and Covenants 17:1). This compass or director pointed the way that Lehi and his caravan should go (see 1 Nephi 16:10), even "a straight course to the promised land" (Alma 37:44). The pointers in the Liahona operated "according to the faith and diligence and heed" (1 Nephi 16:28) of the travelers and failed to work when family members were contentious, rude, slothful, or unrepentant (see 1 Nephi 18:12, 21; Alma 37:41, 43).

The compass also provided a means whereby Lehi and his family could obtain greater "understanding concerning the ways of the Lord" (1 Nephi 16:29). Thus, the primary purposes of the Liahona were to provide both direction and instruction during a long and demanding journey, and it worked according to the principles of faith and diligence.

Just as Lehi and his family were blessed by the Liahona in ancient times, the covenants and ordinances of the Savior's restored gospel direct and instruct us during our mortal journey. The cardinal direction for all of us in mortality is to come unto and be perfected in Christ (see 3 Nephi 12:20; Moroni 10:32–33). Our covenants and ordinances help us to look to, learn from, always remember, and strive to become more like Him.

In a world of increasing confusion, disorder, and commotion, covenants and ordinances are essential to help us maintain a proper focus upon the Savior and His doctrine—regardless of our challenges and circumstances. And covenants and ordinances that are honored steadfastly, remembered always, and written "with the Spirit of the living God . . . in fleshy tables of the heart" (2 Corinthians 3:3) provide purpose, joy, and the assurance of blessings in mortality and for eternity.

COVENANTS, ORDINANCES, STRENGTH, AND POWER

The covenants and ordinances of salvation and exaltation administered in the Lord's restored Church are far more than nice ideas or mere symbolic rituals. Rather, they are the authorized channels through which we can receive the blessings and powers of heaven. The Lord revealed that "this greater priesthood administereth the gospel and holdeth the key of the mysteries of the kingdom, even the key of the knowledge of God.

"Therefore, in the ordinances thereof, the power of godliness is manifest.

"And without the ordinances thereof, and the authority of the priesthood, the power of godliness is not manifest unto men in the flesh" (Doctrine and Covenants 84:19–21).

We can learn important lessons about covenants and ordinances as sources of strength and power by considering the function of a Wi-Fi signal booster. A strong Wi-Fi connection and access to the Internet are practical necessities for many people in the technology-oriented world in which we live. A poor connection can result from a transmitter or router being out of range in specific rooms or by obstructions, such as furniture or thick walls, which interfere with the signal.

A Wi-Fi booster receives and amplifies an existing signal and then transmits the stronger signal. As a result, the coverage area of a network is enlarged significantly, obstructions are reduced or eliminated, and the Wi-Fi signal reaches the far corners of an office or home.

In a similar way, receiving, remembering, and honoring our covenants and ordinances enable the power of godliness to come into our lives, strengthen us to press forward and overcome the various obstructions we encounter on the covenant path, and enlarge our capacity to reach out to, serve, and bless other people.

Consider, for example, the withdrawal of the Latter-day Saints from Nauvoo in 1846. This exodus caused unimaginable hardship for these devoted disciples, and many sought shelter in camps along the Mississippi River. When word reached Brigham Young about the condition of these exiles, he immediately sent a letter encouraging the brethren to help—reminding them of the covenant made in the Nauvoo Temple. He counseled: "Now is the time for labor. Let the fire of the covenant which you made in the house of the Lord burn in your hearts, like flame unquenchable."[2] Within days, "wagons, ox teams, food, and other supplies" were rolling eastward to rescue the struggling Saints.[3]

What was it that gave those early Church members such strength? What fueled their devotion and enabled them to press forward in overwhelmingly adverse conditions? It was the fire of the temple covenants and ordinances that burned in their hearts. It was their commitment to "worship, and honorably hold a name and standing" (Doctrine and Covenants 109:24) in the house of the Lord.

President M. Russell Ballard explained: "Sometimes we are tempted to let our lives be governed more by convenience than by covenant. It is not always convenient to live gospel standards and stand up for truth and testify of the Restoration. It usually is not convenient to share the gospel with others. It isn't always convenient to respond to a calling in the Church, especially one that stretches our abilities. Opportunities to serve others in meaningful ways, as we have covenanted to do, rarely come at convenient times. But there is no spiritual power in living by convenience. The power comes as we keep our covenants. As we look at the lives of these early Saints, we see that their covenants were the primary force in their lives."[4]

In their extremity, these devoted disciples in Nauvoo were keenly aware of their dependence upon God and trusted in Him for deliverance. And I believe they understood that sacred covenants and priesthood ordinances received worthily and remembered continually are the heavenly means through which we have access to the power of godliness and all the blessings made available through the Savior's Atonement.

I cannot emphasize strongly enough this truth: These remarkable gifts and opportunities are available to every covenant-making and covenant-keeping member of The Church of Jesus Christ of Latter-day Saints. I testify and witness that all these choice blessings are available to each of you—individually and personally.

I invite you to read, study, and ponder the Book of Mormon with increased attention to the importance of sacred covenants and ordinances. The Book of Mormon restores knowledge about the role and importance of God's covenants with His sons and daughters on the earth. In fact, the title page itself contains a statement by Moroni regarding the purposes of the book: "to show unto the remnant of the house of Israel what great things the Lord hath done for their fathers; and that they may know the covenants of the Lord" (Book of Mormon title page).

With the Book of Mormon prophet Jacob, I joyfully declare that "my soul delighteth in the covenants of the Lord" (2 Nephi 11:5).

CHAPTER 3

ARMED WITH THE POWER
OF GOD IN GREAT GLORY

I invite you to reflect often and sincerely on the promise that we can receive the "power of God in great glory" and consider the blessings promised to covenant-keeping disciples of Jesus Christ. For example, Nephi "beheld the power of the Lamb of God, that it descended upon the saints of the church of the Lamb and *upon the covenant people of the Lord,*" who, though their "numbers were few" and "dominions . . . small," "were *armed with righteousness and with the power of God in great glory*" (1 Nephi 14:12, 14; emphasis added).

The phrase "armed with righteousness and with the power of God in great glory" is not simply a nice idea or an example of beautiful scriptural language. Rather, these blessings are readily evident in the lives of countless latter-day disciples of the Lord.

Elder D. Todd Christofferson explained, "In all the ordinances, especially those of the temple, we are endowed with power from on high. This 'power of godliness' [Doctrine and Covenants 84:20] comes in the person and by the influence of the Holy Ghost. The gift of the Holy Ghost is part of the new and everlasting covenant. It is an essential part of our baptism, the baptism of the Spirit. It is the messenger of grace by which the blood of Christ is applied to take away our sins and sanctify us (see 2 Nephi 31:17). It is the gift by which Adam was 'quickened in the inner man' (Moses 6:65). It was by the Holy Ghost that the ancient Apostles endured all that they endured and by their priesthood keys carried the gospel to the known world of their day."[1]

My assignments as a member of the Twelve take me all over the world. And I have been blessed to meet and learn memorable lessons from many of you. I testify that the covenant people of the Lord today indeed are armed with righteousness and with the power of God in great glory. I have witnessed faith, courage, perspective, persistence, and joy that extend far beyond mortal capacity—and that only God could provide.

I witnessed the righteousness and power of God in great glory, received through faithfulness to covenants and ordinances, in the life of a young Church member who was partially paralyzed in a horrific automobile accident. After this individual's grueling months of recovery and adapting to a new lifestyle with restricted mobility, I met and talked with this stalwart soul. During our conversation I asked, "What has this experience helped you to learn?" The immediate response was, "I am not sad. I am not mad. And everything will be OK."

I witnessed the righteousness and power of God in great glory, received through faithfulness to covenants and ordinances, in the lives of newly baptized and confirmed members of the Church. These converts were eager to learn and serve, willing but often unsure about how to set aside old habits and strong traditions, and yet joyful to become "fellowcitizens with the saints, and of the household of God" (Ephesians 2:19).

I witnessed the righteousness and power of God in great glory, received through faithfulness to covenants and ordinances, in the lives of a family who cared tenderly for a spouse and parent with a terminal disease. These valiant disciples described times that their family felt all alone—and times they knew the hand of the Lord was lifting and strengthening them. This family expressed sincere gratitude for the difficult mortal experiences that allow us to grow and become more like our Heavenly Father and our Redeemer, Jesus Christ. God succored and blessed this family with the companionship of the Holy Ghost and made their home as sacred a place of refuge as the temple.

I witnessed the righteousness and power of God in great glory, received through faithfulness to covenants and ordinances, in the life of a Church member who experienced the heartache of divorce. This sister's spiritual and emotional distress was heightened by a sense of unfairness associated with her spouse's violation of covenants and the breakup of their marriage. She wanted justice and accountability.

As this faithful woman was struggling with all that had happened to her, she studied and pondered the Savior's Atonement more intently and intensely than ever before in her life. Gradually, a deeper understanding of Christ's redemptive mission distilled upon her soul—His suffering for our sins and also for our pains, weaknesses, disappointments, and anguish. And she was inspired to ask herself a penetrating question: since the price already has been paid for those sins, would you demand that the price be paid twice? She realized that such a requirement would be neither just nor merciful.

This woman learned that binding herself to God and the Savior through covenants and ordinances can heal the wounds caused by another person's unrighteous exercise of moral agency and enabled her to find the capacity to forgive and receive peace, mercy, and love.

President Russell M. Nelson taught, "The reward for keeping covenants with God is heavenly power—power that strengthens us to withstand our trials, temptations, and heartaches better. This power eases our way. Those who live the higher laws of Jesus Christ have access to His higher power. Thus, covenant keepers are entitled to a special kind of *rest* that comes to them through their covenantal relationship with God. . . .

"Entering into a covenant relationship with God binds us to

Him in a way that makes *everything* about life easier. Please do not misunderstand me: I did *not* say that making covenants makes life *easy*. In fact, expect opposition, because the adversary does not want you to discover the power of Jesus Christ. But yoking yourself with the Savior means you have access to *His* strength and redeeming power."[2]

I testify and promise that honoring covenants arms us with righteousness and with the power of God in great glory.

CHAPTER 4

THE PROMISE OF DELIVERANCE
AND ENABLING STRENGTH

———————◆———————

Another grand promise and blessing of binding ourselves to
Heavenly Father and the Savior through covenants is that
we are not, and never need be, alone. We can press forward joyfully in our daily lives with heavenly help. Through the Savior's
Atonement and our covenants, we receive strength to do and become what we simply could not do and become relying only on
our limited mortal capacity.

I testify that this declaration of the Lord is true: "Therefore,
continue your journey and let your hearts rejoice; for behold, and
lo, *I am with you* even unto the end" (Doctrine and Covenants
100:12; emphasis added).

In many of the uncertainties and challenges we encounter
in our lives, God requires us to do our best, to act and not be
acted upon (see 2 Nephi 2:26), and to trust in Him. We may
not see angels, hear heavenly voices, or receive overwhelming

spiritual impressions. We frequently may press forward hoping and praying—but without absolute assurance—that we are acting in accordance with God's will. But as we honor our covenants and keep the commandments, as we strive ever more consistently to do good and to become better, we can walk with the confidence that God will guide our steps. And we can speak with the assurance that God will inspire our utterances. This is in part the meaning of the scripture that declares, "Then shall thy confidence wax strong in the presence of God" (Doctrine and Covenants 121:45).

THE STRENGTHENING POWER OF THE ATONEMENT OF JESUS CHRIST

Reflect again on the Lord's uniquely individual invitation to "take my yoke upon you" (Matthew 11:29). Making and keeping sacred covenants yokes us to and with the Lord Jesus Christ. In essence, the Savior is beckoning us to rely upon and pull together with Him, even though our best efforts are not equal to and cannot be compared with His. As we trust in and pull our load with Him during the journey of mortality, truly His yoke is easy and His burden is light (see Matthew 11:30).

Consider the example in the Book of Mormon as Amulon persecuted Alma and his people. The voice of the Lord came to these disciples in their afflictions: "Lift up your heads and be of good comfort, for I know of the covenant which ye have made unto me; and I will covenant with my people and deliver them out of bondage" (Mosiah 24:13).

Note the centrality of covenants to the promise of deliverance. Covenants received and honored with integrity and ordinances performed by proper priesthood authority are necessary to receive all of the blessings made available through the Atonement of Jesus Christ. For in the ordinances of the priesthood, the power of godliness, including the blessings of the Atonement, is manifest unto men and women in the flesh (see Doctrine and Covenants 84:20–21).

Recall the Savior's statement "For my yoke is easy, and my burden is light" (Matthew 11:30) as we consider the next verse in the account of Alma and his people.

"And I will also ease the burdens which are put upon your shoulders, that even you cannot feel them upon your backs" (Mosiah 24:14).

Many of us may assume this scripture is suggesting that a burden suddenly and permanently will be taken away. The next verse, however, describes how the burden was eased.

"And now it came to pass that the burdens which were laid upon Alma and his brethren were made light; yea, *the Lord did strengthen them* that they could bear up their burdens with ease, and they did submit cheerfully and with patience to all the will of the Lord" (Mosiah 24:15; emphasis added).

The challenges and difficulties were not immediately removed from the people. But Alma and his followers were strengthened, and their increased capacity made the burdens lighter. These good people were empowered through the Atonement of Jesus Christ to *act* as agents (see Doctrine and Covenants 58:26–29) and impact their circumstances. And "in the strength of the Lord" (Words of Mormon 1:14; Mosiah 9:17; 10:10; Alma 20:4), Alma and his people were directed to safety in the land of Zarahemla.

Not only does the Atonement of Jesus Christ overcome the effects of the Fall of Adam and Eve and make possible the remission of our individual sins and transgressions, but His Atonement also enables us to do good and become better in ways that stretch far beyond our mortal capacities. Most of us know that when we do things wrong and need help to overcome the effects of sin in our lives, we can become clean through the Savior's redeeming power. But do we also understand that the Atonement is for faithful men and women who are obedient, worthy, and conscientious and who are striving to become better and serve more faithfully? I wonder if we fail to fully acknowledge this strengthening aspect of the Atonement in our lives and mistakenly believe we must carry our load all alone—through sheer grit, willpower, and discipline and with our obviously limited capacities.

It is one thing to know that Jesus Christ came to the earth to *die* for us. But we also need to appreciate that the Lord desires, through His Atonement and by the power of the Holy Ghost, to *enliven* us—not only to guide but also to strengthen and heal us.

THE SAVIOR SUCCORS HIS PEOPLE

Alma explains why and how the Savior can enable us:

"And he shall go forth, suffering pains and afflictions and temptations of every kind; and this that the word might be fulfilled which saith he will take upon him the pains and the sicknesses of his people.

"And he will take upon him death, that he may loose the bands of death which bind his people; and he will take upon him their infirmities, that his bowels may be filled with mercy, according to the flesh, that he may know according to the flesh how to succor his people according to their infirmities" (Alma 7:11–12).

Thus, the Savior has suffered not just for our sins and iniquities—but also for our physical pains and anguish, our weaknesses and shortcomings, our fears and frustrations, our disappointments and discouragement, our regrets and remorse, our despair and desperation, the injustices and inequities we experience, and the emotional distresses that beset us.

There is no physical pain, no spiritual wound, no anguish of soul or heartache, no infirmity or weakness you or I ever confront in mortality that the Savior did not experience first. In a moment of weakness we may cry out, "No one knows what it is like. No one understands." But the Son of God perfectly knows and understands, for He has felt and borne our individual burdens. And because of His infinite and eternal sacrifice (see Alma

34:14), He has perfect empathy and can extend to us His arm of mercy. He can reach out, touch, succor, heal, and strengthen us to be more than we could ever be and help us to do that which we could never do relying only upon our own power. Indeed, His yoke is easy and His burden is light.

The unique burdens in each of our lives help us to rely upon the merits, mercy, and grace of the Holy Messiah (see 2 Nephi 2:8). I testify and promise the Savior will help us to bear up our burdens with ease (see Mosiah 24:15). As we are yoked with Him through sacred covenants and receive the enabling power of His Atonement in our lives, we increasingly will seek to understand and live according to His will. We also will pray for the strength to learn from, change, or accept our circumstances rather than praying relentlessly for God to change our circumstances according to our will. We will become agents who act rather than objects that are acted upon (see 2 Nephi 2:14). We will be blessed with spiritual traction to "press forward" in our efforts to receive the spiritual gift of an immovable faith (2 Nephi 31:20).

CHAPTER 5

THE CAPACITY TO "HEED NOT"

One hymn that has blessed my life in remarkable ways is "Let Us All Press On." Recently I have been pondering and learning about a specific phrase in the refrain of that hymn: "*We will heed not* what the wicked may say, But the Lord alone we will obey."[1]

We will heed not.

As I sing "Let Us All Press On," I often think of the people in Lehi's vision pressing forward on the path that led to the tree of life who were not merely "clinging to" (1 Nephi 8:24) but were "continually holding fast to the rod of iron, until they came forth and fell down and partook of the fruit of the tree" (1 Nephi 8:30). Lehi described multitudes in the great and spacious building that were pointing "the finger of scorn at [him] and those . . . partaking of the fruit" (1 Nephi 8:33). His response to the jeers and insults is magnificent and memorable: "*But we heeded them not*" (1 Nephi 8:33; emphasis added).

Each of us prayerfully should consider how we can be strengthened through our faith in the Savior and the covenants and ordinances of His restored gospel to "heed not" the evil influences and mocking voices of the contemporary world in which we live.

HEED NOT

The word *heed* suggests taking notice of or paying attention to someone or something. Thus, the lyrics of the hymn "Let Us All Press On" admonish us to make an affirmative decision to pay no attention to "what the wicked may say." And Lehi and the people with him who were partaking of the fruit of the tree provide a strong example of not paying attention to the mocking and scorn that so frequently come from the great and spacious building.

The doctrine of Christ written "with the Spirit of the living God . . . in fleshy tables of [our hearts]" (2 Corinthians 3:3) increases our capacity to "heed not" the many distractions, taunts, and diversions in our fallen world. For example, faith focused in and on the Lord Jesus Christ fortifies us with spiritual strength. Faith in the Redeemer is a principle of action and of power. As we act in accordance with the truths of His gospel, we are blessed with the spiritual capacity to press forward through the challenges of mortality while focusing on the joys the Savior offers to us.

Truly, "if we do what's right we have no need to fear, for the Lord, our helper, will ever be near."[2]

I frankly do not have the ability to describe adequately the precise nature and power of our covenant connection with the resurrected and living Son of God. But I witness that the connections with Him and Heavenly Father are real and are the ultimate sources of assurance, peace, joy, and the spiritual strength that enable us to "fear not, though the enemy deride."[3] As covenant-making and covenant-keeping disciples of Jesus Christ, we can be blessed to take "courage, for the Lord is on our side"[4] and pay no attention to evil influences and secular scoffing.

HOLDING FAST TO THE IRON ROD

We can receive the capacity and power to "heed not" through our covenant connection with God and Jesus Christ. And this bond is strengthened as we continually hold fast to the rod of iron. But as Nephi's brethren asked, "What meaneth the rod of iron which our father saw . . . ?

"And [Nephi] said unto them that it was the *word of God*; and whoso would hearken unto *the word of God*, and would *hold fast unto it*, they would never perish; neither could the temptations and the fiery darts of the adversary overpower them unto blindness, to lead them away to destruction" (1 Nephi 15:23–24; emphasis added).

Interestingly, the Apostle John described Jesus Christ as the Word.[5]

"In the beginning was *the Word*, and *the Word* was with God, and *the Word* was God. . . .

"All things were made by him; and without him was not any thing made that was made. . . .

"And *the Word* was made flesh, and dwelt among us, (and we beheld his glory, the glory as of the only begotten of the Father,) full of grace and truth" (John 1:1, 3, 14; emphasis added).

Therefore, one of the names of Jesus Christ is "the Word."[6]

In addition, the eighth article of faith states, "We believe the Bible to be *the word of God* as far as it is translated correctly; we also believe the Book of Mormon to be *the word of God*" (Articles of Faith 1:8; emphasis added).

Thus, the teachings of the Savior, as recorded in the holy scriptures, also are "the word."

Let me suggest that holding fast to the word of God entails (1) remembering, honoring, and strengthening the personal connection we have with the Savior and His Father through the covenants and ordinances of the restored gospel and (2) prayer-fully, earnestly, and consistently using the holy scriptures and the teachings of living prophets and apostles as sure sources of re-vealed truth. As we are bound and "hold fast" to the Lord and are transformed by living His doctrine (see 2 Corinthians 5:17;

Mosiah 3:19; 5:2; 27:25–26; Alma 5:49; Moroni 10:32), I promise that individually and collectively we will be blessed to "stand in holy places, and shall not be moved" (Doctrine and Covenants 45:32). If we abide in Christ, then He will abide in and walk with us (see John 15:4–8; Doctrine and Covenants 50:41–43; Moses 6:33–34, 39). Surely, "in the days of trial his Saints he will cheer, and prosper the cause of truth."[7]

Press on. Hold fast. Heed not.

I witness that fidelity to the covenants and ordinances of the Savior's restored gospel enables us to *press on* in the work of the Lord, to *hold fast* to Him as the Word of God, and to *heed not* the allurements of the adversary. Our covenant connection with the Lord anchors our foundations to Jesus Christ.

BY STUDY AND ALSO BY FAITH– ASK, SEEK, AND KNOCK

CHAPTER 6

LEARNING FOR OURSELVES

The spiritual foundation of our lives can be strengthened and become ever firmer as we follow this sacred invitation from our Savior: "Ask, and it shall be given unto you; seek, and ye shall find; knock, and it shall be opened unto you" (3 Nephi 14:7).

But what should we be asking for and seeking after? What do we hope shall be opened unto us?

I believe discovering the answers to these important questions is quite straightforward. Obtaining answers *for ourselves* is the pursuit of a lifetime.

As young Joseph Smith returned to his home from the Sacred Grove immediately after the appearance of the Father and the Son, he spoke first with his mother. As he "leaned up to the fireplace, [his] mother inquired what the matter was. [Joseph] replied, 'Never mind, all is well—I am well enough off.' [He] then said to [his] mother, '*I have learned for myself . . .*'" (Joseph Smith—History 1:20; emphasis added).

We should ask, seek, and knock to learn about and understand *for ourselves* the most basic and fundamental truths of the restored gospel of Jesus Christ.

President Heber C. Kimball said, "Suppose you had only one seed to plant, and that seed was an acorn, and you spend your time in cultivating it till it comes forth a great and mighty tree, branching forth with many branches and bearing fruit abundantly after its own kind. So it is with the first principles of the Gospel, they branch out in all directions, unfolding new light continually."[1] We can never study too often or too much the fundamental principles of the restored gospel of Jesus Christ because repetition facilitates revelation in a powerful way.

Hyrum Smith said, "Preach the first principles of the Gospel—preach them over again: you will find that day after day new ideas and additional light concerning them will be revealed to you. You can enlarge upon them so as to comprehend them clearly. You will then be able to make them more plainly understood by those [you] teach."[2]

Repetition invites the Holy Ghost to renew, enrich, and enlarge the knowledge we already have obtained; it also can bring new knowledge and understanding into our minds and hearts. Thus, repetition is a vehicle through which the Holy Ghost can enlighten our minds, influence our hearts, and enlarge our understanding.

CORRECT PRINCIPLES

It is impossible to exercise faith in something that is false. I cannot emphasize strongly enough the importance of *learning for ourselves* the basic, simple, and correct principles of the restored gospel of Jesus Christ as found in the holy scriptures and the teachings of living prophets and apostles. Only a correct understanding of the Father's eternal plan of happiness and the Savior's Atonement and His gospel can provide the strong spiritual foundation that will enable us to stand firm and steadfast in the latter days.

All of us should avoid speculating about subjects on which little or nothing has been revealed, perpetuating unsubstantiated claims and rumors, and substituting personal opinions and experiences for the word of God. We individually should pay the price to learn and understand the doctrine and principles for ourselves by the power of the Holy Ghost: we must "own it!"

President Russell M. Nelson declared, "The foundation of this Church was forged long before the world was. It is strong. It is true. It is eternal. The foundation of one's individual faith, if anchored firmly to eternal truth, allows each of us to reach upward with an eternal perspective."[3]

INDIVIDUAL AND PERSONAL

As I visit with members of the Church around the world, I often ask them this question: what helps you to ignore worldly influences, mocking, and scorn? Their answers are most instructive.

Valiant members often highlight the importance of inviting the power of the Holy Ghost into their lives through meaningful scripture study, fervent prayer, and proper preparation to participate in the ordinance of the sacrament. Also mentioned frequently are the spiritual support of faithful family members and trusted friends, the vital lessons learned through ministering and serving in the Lord's restored Church, and the capacity to discern the absolute emptiness of anything in or coming from the great and spacious building.

I have noted in these responses a particular pattern that is especially significant. First and foremost, these disciples have firm testimonies of Heavenly Father's plan of happiness and the role of Jesus Christ as our Redeemer and Savior. And second, their spiritual knowledge and conviction are *individual, personal, and specific*; they are not general and abstract. I listen to these devoted souls speak of covenants providing strength to overcome opposition and their connection with the living Lord supporting them through times both good and bad. To these individuals, Jesus Christ indeed is a personal Savior.

I promise that by the power of the Holy Ghost, you can

know and feel gospel truths are for you—for you individually and personally.

President Heber C. Kimball said: "This Church has before it many close places through which it will have to pass before the work of God is crowned with victory. . . . The time will come when no man nor woman will be able to endure on borrowed light. Each will have to be guided by the light within himself. If you do not have it, how can you stand?"[4]

If we do not put forth the effort to learn the truths of the restored gospel for ourselves, then the foundation of our testimony of Him and His glorious latter-day work is built upon sand. We cannot rely exclusively upon or borrow gospel light and knowledge from other people—even those whom we love and trust.

UNDERSTANDING IN OUR HEARTS

To develop personal, abiding testimonies, you and I must apply our hearts to understanding. As I read and study each of the standard works, I am intrigued that the word *understanding* is commonly described in relation to the heart. Two verses in the Book of Mormon illustrate this connection:

"Ye have not applied your *hearts* to *understanding*; therefore, ye have not been wise" (Mosiah 12:27; emphasis added).

"And the multitude did hear and do bear record; and their hearts were open and they did *understand* in their *hearts* the words which he prayed" (3 Nephi 19:33; emphasis added).

I find it most interesting in these and many other verses that understanding is linked primarily to the heart. Note that we are not explicitly counseled to apply our minds to understanding. Obviously, we must use our minds and our rational capacity to obtain and evaluate information and to reach appropriate conclusions and judgments. But perhaps the scriptures are suggesting to us that reason and "the arm of flesh" (Doctrine and Covenants 1:19) are not sufficient to produce true understanding. Thus, *understanding*, as the word is used in the scriptures, does not refer solely or even primarily to intellectual or cognitive comprehension. Rather, understanding occurs when what we know in our minds is confirmed as true in our hearts by the witness of the Holy Ghost.

The spiritual gift of revelation most typically operates as thoughts and feelings put into our minds and hearts by the Holy Ghost (see Doctrine and Covenants 8:2–3; 100:5–8). And as testimony and conviction move from our heads to our hearts, we no longer have just information or knowledge—we begin to understand and seek after the mighty change of heart. Understanding, then, is the result of revelation; it is a spiritual gift, it is a prerequisite to conversion, and it entices us to more consistently live in accordance with the principles we are learning.

"And now . . . I desire that ye shall *plant this word in your hearts*, and as it beginneth to swell even so nourish it by your faith. And behold, *it will become a tree*, springing up *in you* unto everlasting life. And then may God grant unto you that your burdens may be light, through the joy of his Son. And even all this can ye do if ye will" (Alma 33:23; emphasis added).

The seed we should strive to plant in our hearts is the word—even the life, mission, and doctrine of Jesus Christ. And as the word is nourished by faith, it can become a tree springing up *in us* unto everlasting life (see Alma 26:13).

What was the symbolism of the tree in Lehi's vision? The tree can be considered a representation of Jesus Christ.[5]

My beloved brothers and sisters, is the Word in us? Are the truths of the Savior's gospel written in the fleshy tables of our hearts? (see 2 Corinthians 3:3). Are we coming unto and gradually becoming more like Him? Is the tree of Christ growing in us? Are we striving to become "new creature[s]" (2 Corinthians 5:17) in Him?[6]

Perhaps this miraculous potential inspired Alma to ask: "Have ye spiritually been born of God? Have ye received his image in your countenances? Have ye experienced this mighty change in your hearts?" (Alma 5:14).

I pray that you and I will apply our hearts to understanding and continue to ask, seek, and knock with increased focus, a sincere heart, and real intent. As we do so, we will be blessed by the power of the Holy Ghost to know the truth of all things that are essential to our salvation and exaltation. We can experience a mighty change in our hearts and receive His image in our countenances—blessings and evidence that our spiritual foundations are anchored to Jesus Christ.

CHAPTER 7

LINE UPON LINE AND PRECEPT UPON PRECEPT

Typically as disciples of Jesus Christ, we learn the truths of His gospel "line upon line and precept upon precept, here a little and there a little; and blessed are those who hearken unto [His] precepts, and lend an ear unto [His] counsel, for they shall learn wisdom; for unto him that receiveth [He] will give more; and from them that shall say, We have enough, from them shall be taken away even that which they have" (2 Nephi 28:30).

The Lord also emphasized the importance of an incremental and gradual pattern of gospel learning in a revelation given to the Prophet Joseph Smith in 1831 in Kirtland, Ohio. "Wherefore, be not weary in well-doing, for ye are laying the foundation of a great work. And out of *small things* proceedeth that which is great" (Doctrine and Covenants 64:33; emphasis added).

As we become more spiritually mature and increasingly stead-fast and immovable, we focus upon and strive to understand the foundational doctrine of the restored gospel of Jesus Christ. Disciples who are steadfast and immovable do not become fanatics or extremists, are not overzealous, and are not preoccupied with misguided gospel hobbies.

President Joseph F. Smith emphasized: "We frequently look about us and see people who incline to extremes, who are fanatical. We may be sure that this class of people do not understand the gospel. They have forgotten, if they ever knew, that it is very unwise to take a fragment of truth and treat it as if it were the whole thing."[1]

Let me repeat and reinforce this first great blessing associated with being a steadfast and immovable disciple of the Savior: such a follower of Christ consistently is focused upon and striving to understand the foundational doctrine of the restored gospel.

Second, as we become more spiritually mature and increasingly steadfast and immovable, we are less prone to zealous and exaggerated spurts of spirituality followed by extended periods of slackness.

In order to better understand this principle, please consider Aesop's fable "The Hare and the Tortoise." After being taunted repeatedly for being slow, the Tortoise challenged the Hare to a race. As the race began, the two started off together. However, the Hare ran rapidly toward the goal and, seeing that he could easily win, lay down and fell asleep a short distance in front of the finish line. The Tortoise maintained a slow but steady and consistent pace toward the finish line. When the Hare awoke from his nap, he started running as fast as he could, only to find that the Tortoise had won the race. The Tortoise is a classic illustration of steadiness and persistence. The Hare, on the other hand, is an example of a "spurter"—one who is given to short bursts of spectacular effort followed by frequent and lengthy periods of rest.

We can learn much about the nature and importance of the spiritual pattern of "small things" from the technique of drip irrigation that is used in many gardens and in agricultural areas throughout the world. Drip irrigation is sometimes called trickle irrigation and involves dripping water onto the soil at very low rates from a system of small plastic pipes fitted with outlets called emitters or drippers. Unlike surface and sprinkler irrigation that involves flooding or gushing or spraying large quantities of water where it may not be needed, drip irrigation applies water close to a plant so that only the part of the soil in which the roots grow is wetted.

With drip irrigation, applications of water are more focused and more frequent than with the other methods. The steady drips of water sink deep into the ground and provide a high moisture level in the soil wherein plants can flourish. In like manner, if you and I are focused on and frequent in receiving consistent drops of spiritual nourishment, then gospel roots can sink deep into our souls, can become firmly established and grounded, and can produce extraordinary and delicious fruit.

A big spurt may appear to be impressive in the short run, but steadiness in small things over time is far more effective and far less dangerous and produces far better results. Three consecutive days of fasting ultimately may not be as spiritually efficacious as three successive months of appropriate fasting and worship on the designated fast Sunday. A great attempt to pray one time for five hours likely will not produce the spiritual results of meaningful morning and evening prayer offered consistently over five weeks. And a single, great scripture-reading marathon cannot produce the spiritual impact of steady scripture study across many months—of many small and simple things done consistently well.

In a gospel sense, you and I need to become intelligent drip irrigators and avoid sporadic and shallow spiritual spurting. We can avoid or overcome unsustainable spiritual spurting as we employ the Lord's pattern of small and simple things and become truly intelligent irrigators. The spiritual pattern of small and simple things bringing forth great things produces firmness and steadfastness, deepening devotion, and more complete conversion to the Lord Jesus Christ and His gospel.

Elder Neal A. Maxwell explained: "Measured steadiness is more efficient than spurts and then a slackening. Further, we are less apt to 'wear away' in prudent persistence than in a combination of breathlessness and ease. Sometimes we may reward our breathlessness with a respite that turns into a permanent repose;

we do this by reflecting on all that we have done up to now and how it is surely now someone else's turn."[2]

President Spencer W. Kimball taught about the importance of small and simple things in our spiritual development and progress. In explicating the parable of the ten virgins he stated:

"The foolish [virgins] asked the others to share their oil, but spiritual preparedness cannot be shared in an instant. The wise had to go, else the bridegroom would have gone unwelcomed. They needed all their oil for themselves; they could not save the foolish. The responsibility was each for [herself].

"This was not selfishness or unkindness. The kind of oil that is needed to illuminate the way and light up the darkness is not shareable. How can one share obedience to the principle of tithing; a mind at peace from righteous living; an accumulation of knowledge? How can one share faith or testimony? How can one share attitudes or chastity, or the experience of a mission? How can one share temple privileges? Each must obtain that kind of oil for himself.

"The foolish virgins were not averse to buying oil. They knew they should have oil. They merely procrastinated, not knowing when the bridegroom would come.

"In the parable, oil can be purchased at the market. In our lives the oil of preparedness is accumulated drop by drop in righteous living. Attendance at sacrament meetings adds oil to our lamps, drop by drop over the years. Fasting, family prayer, home teaching [or ministering visits today], control of bodily appetites, preaching the gospel, studying the scriptures—each act of dedication and obedience is a drop added to our store. Deeds of kindness, payment of offerings and tithes, chaste thoughts and actions, marriage in the covenant for eternity—these, too, contribute importantly to the oil with which we can at midnight refuel our exhausted lamps."[3]

The key lesson for us to learn from the parable of the ten virgins is that deliberate and consistent preparation and performance provide essential oil for our lamps. Line upon line and precept upon precept—by small and simple things are great things brought to pass.

CHAPTER 8

THE SCRIPTURES:
A RESERVOIR OF LIVING WATER

E arnestly asking, seeking, and knocking can open the floodgates of the scriptures as a spiritual reservoir, enlighten our understanding through His Spirit, and produce a depth of gratitude and a degree of spiritual commitment that can be received in no other way. Such searching enables us to build upon the "rock of our Redeemer" (Helaman 5:12) and to withstand the winds of wickedness in these latter days.

LIVING WATER

What is the most valuable substance or commodity in the world? We might initially think that gold, oil, or diamonds have the greatest worth. But of all the minerals, metals, gems, and solvents found on and in the earth, the most valuable is water.

Life springs from water. Life is sustained by water. Water is the medium required to perform the various functions associated with all known forms of life. Our physical bodies are approximately two-thirds water. Whereas a person can survive for many days or even weeks without food, an individual will usually die in only three or four days without water. Most of the world's great centers of population are situated near sources of fresh water. Simply stated, life could not exist without the availability of and access to adequate supplies of clean water.

The scriptures contain the words of Christ and are a reservoir of living water to which we have ready access and from which we can drink deeply and long. You and I must look to and come unto Christ, who is "the fountain of living waters" (1 Nephi 11:25; compare Ether 8:26, 12:28), by *reading* (see Mosiah 1:5), *studying* (see Doctrine and Covenants 26:1), *searching* (see John 5:39; Alma 17:2), and *feasting* (see 2 Nephi 32:3) upon the words of Christ as contained in the holy scriptures. By so doing, we can receive both spiritual direction and protection during our mortal journey.

Not only are we blessed to have these scriptures so readily available to us today, but we also have the responsibility to use them consistently and effectively and to drink deeply from the reservoir of living water.

OBTAINING LIVING WATER FROM THE SCRIPTURAL RESERVOIR

I want to review with you three basic ways or methods of obtaining living water from the scriptural reservoir: (1) *reading* the scriptures from beginning to end, (2) *studying* the scriptures by topic, and (3) *searching* the scriptures for connections, patterns, and themes. Each of these approaches can help satisfy our spiritual thirst if we invite the companionship and assistance of the Holy Ghost as we read, study, and search.

Reading a book of scripture from beginning to end initiates the flow of living water into our lives by introducing us to important stories, gospel doctrine, and timeless principles. This approach also enables us to learn about major characters in the scriptures and the sequence, timing, and context of events and teachings. Reading the written word in this way exposes us to the breadth of a volume of scripture. This is the first and most fundamental way of obtaining living water.

Studying by topic typically follows, grows out of, and builds upon our reading of the scriptures from beginning to end. For example, as we read the Book of Mormon, we may identify and seek to find answers to important doctrinal and practical questions such as these:

- What is faith in the Savior?
- Why is faith in Jesus Christ the first principle of the gospel?
- Why and how does faith in the Redeemer lead to repentance?
- How does the Savior's Atonement strengthen me to do things in my daily life that I could never do with my own limited capacity and in my own strength?

Focusing upon such questions and studying by topic, using the Topical Guide or Guide to the Scriptures and index to the triple combination, allow us to dig into and explore the depth of the scriptures and obtain a much richer spiritual knowledge. This approach increases the rate at which living water flows into our lives.

Both reading from beginning to end and studying by topic are prerequisites to the third basic method of obtaining living water from the scriptural reservoir. Whereas reading a book of scripture from beginning to end provides a basic breadth of knowledge, studying by topic increases the depth of our knowledge. *Searching* in the revelations for connections, patterns, and themes builds upon and adds to our spiritual knowledge by bringing together and expanding these first two methods; it broadens our perspective and understanding of the plan of salvation.

The Prophet Joseph Smith taught that we should "search the scriptures—search the revelations which we publish, and ask your Heavenly Father, in the name of His Son Jesus Christ, to manifest the truth unto you, and if you do it with an eye single to His glory, nothing doubting, He will answer you by the power of His Holy Spirit. You will then know for yourselves and not from another. You will not then be dependent on man for the knowledge of God."[1]

Let me briefly explain and provide examples of what I mean by connections, patterns, and themes.

Connections

A connection is a relationship or link between ideas, people, things, or events, and the scriptures are full of connections. Consider the relationship between the Eternal Father and His Son, Jesus Christ (see Mosiah 15:1–9); between mercy and grace (see 2 Nephi 9:8); between clean hands and a pure heart (see Psalm 24:4); between a broken heart and a contrite spirit (see 3 Nephi 9:20); between the wheat and the tares (see Doctrine and Covenants 101:65); between knowledge and intelligence (see Doctrine and Covenants 130:18–19); between justification and sanctification (see Doctrine and Covenants 20:30–31); between sheep and goats (see Matthew 25:32–33); between immortality and eternal life (see Moses 1:39); and countless others. Prayerfully identifying, learning about, and pondering such connections—the similarities and differences, for example—is a primary source of living water and yields inspired insights and treasures of hidden knowledge.

Patterns

A pattern is a plan, model, or standard that can be used as a guide for repetitively doing or making something. And the scriptures are full of spiritual patterns. Typically, a scriptural pattern is broader and more comprehensive than a connection. In the Doctrine and Covenants we find patterns for preaching the gospel (see Doctrine and Covenants 50:13–29), for avoiding deception (see Doctrine and Covenants 52:14, 18–19), for constructing houses of the Lord (see Doctrine and Covenants 115:14–16), for establishing cities (see Doctrine and Covenants 94), for organizing priesthood quorums (see Doctrine and Covenants 107:85–100) and high councils (see Doctrine and Covenants 102:12), and for a variety of other purposes. Identifying and studying scriptural patterns is another important source of living water and helps us become acquainted and more familiar with the wisdom and the mind of the Lord (see Doctrine and Covenants 95:13).

Themes

Themes are overarching, recurring, and unifying qualities or ideas, like essential threads woven throughout a text. Generally, scriptural themes are broader and more comprehensive than patterns or connections. In fact, themes provide the background and context for understanding connections and patterns. The process of searching for and identifying scriptural themes leads us to the fundamental doctrine and principles of salvation—to the eternal truths that invite the confirming witness of the Holy Ghost (see 1 John 5:6). This approach to obtaining living water from the scriptural reservoir is the most demanding and rigorous; it also yields the greatest edification and spiritual refreshment. And the scriptures are replete with powerful themes.

For example, the Book of Mormon came forth in this dispensation to "the convincing of the Jew and Gentile that Jesus is the Christ, the Eternal God, manifesting himself unto all nations"

(Book of Mormon title page). The central and recurring theme of the Book of Mormon is the invitation for all to "come unto Christ, and be perfected in him" (Moroni 10:32). The teachings, warnings, admonitions, and episodes in this remarkable book of scripture all focus upon and testify of Jesus the Christ as the Redeemer and our Savior.

Let me suggest a few additional examples of important themes using scriptures from the Book of Mormon:

- "If . . . the children of men keep the commandments of God he doth nourish them, and strengthen them, and provide means whereby they can accomplish the thing which he has commanded them" (1 Nephi 17:3).
- "Press forward with a steadfastness in Christ" (2 Nephi 31:20).
- "Men are, that they might have joy" (2 Nephi 2:25).
- "In the strength of the Lord thou canst do all things" (Alma 20:4).
- "Wickedness never was happiness" (Alma 41:10).

THE BLESSINGS WE CAN RECEIVE

The blessings of knowledge, understanding, revelation, and spiritual exhilaration that we can receive as we read, study, and search the scriptures are marvelous. "Feasting upon the word of Christ" (2 Nephi 31:20) is edifying, exciting, and enjoyable. The word is good, "for it beginneth to enlarge my soul; yea, it beginneth to enlighten my understanding, yea, it beginneth to be delicious to me" (Alma 32:28). "Behold they are written, ye have them before you, therefore search them" (3 Nephi 20:11), and they "shall be in [you] a well of water springing up into everlasting life" (John 4:14).

LEHI'S VISION

The importance of reading, studying, and searching the scriptures is highlighted in several elements of Lehi's vision of the tree of life.

Father Lehi saw several groups of people pressing forward along the strait and narrow path, seeking to obtain the tree and its fruit. The members of each group had entered onto the path through the gate of repentance and baptism by water and had received the gift of the Holy Ghost (see 2 Nephi 31:17–20). The tree of life is the central feature in the dream and is identified in 1 Nephi 11 as a representation of Jesus Christ. The fruit on the tree can be considered a symbol for the blessings of the Savior's Atonement. Interestingly, the major theme of the Book of Mormon, inviting all to come unto Christ, is central in Lehi's vision. Of particular interest is the rod of iron that led to the tree (see 1 Nephi 8:19). The rod of iron is the word of God.

In 1 Nephi 8:21–23, we learn about a group of people who pressed forward and commenced on the path that led to the tree of life. However, as the people encountered the mist of darkness, which represents the temptations of the devil (see 1 Nephi 12:17), they lost their way, they wandered off, and they were lost.

It is important to note that no mention is made about the rod of iron in these verses. Those who ignore or treat lightly the word of God do not have access to that divine compass that points the way to the Savior. Consider that this group obtained the path and pressed forward, exhibiting a measure of faith in Christ and spiritual conviction, but they were diverted by the temptations of the devil and were lost.

In 1 Nephi 8:24–28, we read about a second group of people who obtained the strait and narrow path that led to the tree of life. This group pressed forward through the mist of darkness, clinging to the rod of iron even until they came forth and partook of the fruit of the tree. However, as this second group of people was mocked by the occupants of the great and spacious building, they were ashamed and fell away into forbidden paths and were lost. Please notice that this group is described as *clinging* to the rod of iron.

It is significant that the second group pressed forward with faith and commitment. They also had the added blessing of the rod of iron, *and they were clinging to it!* However, as they were confronted with persecution and adversity, they fell away into forbidden paths and were lost. Even with faith, commitment, and the word of God, this group was lost—perhaps because they only *periodically* read *or* studied *or* searched the scriptures. "Clinging" to the rod of iron suggests to me only occasional "bursts" of study or irregular dipping rather than consistent, ongoing immersion in the word of God.

In verse 30 we read about a third group of people who pressed forward continually holding fast to the rod of iron until they came forth and fell down and partook of the fruit of the tree. The key phrase in this verse is "continually holding fast" to the rod of iron.

The third group also pressed forward with faith and conviction; however, there is no indication that they wandered off, fell into forbidden paths, or were lost. Perhaps this third group of people *consistently* read *and* studied *and* searched the words of Christ. Perhaps it was the constant flow of living water that saved the third group from perishing. This is the group you and I should strive to join (see 1 Nephi 15:23–24).

What, then, is the difference between clinging and holding fast to the rod of iron? Let me suggest that holding fast to the iron rod entails the prayerful and consistent use of all three ways of obtaining living water that we have discussed.

"And it came to pass that I beheld that the rod of iron, which my father had seen, was the word of God, which led to the fountain of living waters, or to the tree of life" (1 Nephi 11:25).

Each of these approaches—reading from beginning to end, studying by topic, and searching for connections, patterns, and themes—is edifying, is instructive, and provides an intermittent portion of the Savior's living water. I believe, however, that the regular use of all three methods produces a more constant flow of living water and is in large measure what it means to hold fast to the rod of iron.

Through normal activity each day, you and I lose a substantial amount of the water that constitutes so much of our physical bodies. Thirst is a demand by the cells of the body for water, and the water in our bodies must be replenished daily. It frankly does not make sense to occasionally "fill up" with water, with long periods of dehydration in between. The same thing is true spiritually. Spiritual thirst is a need for living water. A constant flow of living water is far superior to sporadic sipping.

Are you and I daily reading, studying, and searching the scriptures in a way that enables us to hold fast to the rod of iron—or are you and I merely clinging? Are you and I pressing forward toward the fountain of living waters—relying upon the word of God? These are important questions for each of us to ponder prayerfully.

If you and I will ask, seek, and knock (see Matthew 7:7), always keeping ourselves worthy to learn from the Spirit, then the gates of the spiritual reservoir will open to us and the living water will flow. I witness, I testify, and I promise that this is true.

CHAPTER 9

DOERS OF THE WORD

———◆———

J ust as searching and "feasting" (2 Nephi 31:20) upon the scriptures enable us to hold fast to the rod of iron and become increasingly steadfast and immovable, so does exercising our faith and becoming "doers of the word, and not hearers only" (James 1:22). It is another way we can follow the Savior's invitation to ask, seek, and knock. As we do so, the foundations of our lives are further anchored "to the rock of our Redeemer" (Helaman 5:12).

THE SPIRITUAL EXPERIMENT

Alma explained that "if ye will awake and arouse your faculties, even to an experiment upon my words, and exercise a particle of faith, yea, even if ye can no more than desire to believe, let this desire work in you, even until ye believe in a manner that ye can give place for a portion of my words" (Alma 32:27).

Our faith grows stronger as we accept the invitation to

participate in this spiritual experiment and strive to act in accordance with His teachings and seek gospel learning, "even by study and also by faith" (Doctrine and Covenants 88:118).

When you and I exercise agency by acting in accordance with correct principles, we open our hearts to the Holy Ghost and invite His testifying power and confirming witness. Learning by faith requires spiritual, mental, and physical exertion and not just passive reception. In the sincerity and consistency of faith-inspired action, a person indicates to our Heavenly Father and His Son, Jesus Christ, a willingness to learn and receive instruction from the Holy Ghost.

Faith in the Lord cannot be given, bestowed, transferred, conveyed, or transmitted to us by someone else. But we can begin to focus our faith on and in the Lord Jesus Christ by accepting invitations to ask, seek, and knock for the spiritual gift of faith in Him. We need to remember always that others' best efforts to explain and bear witness of restored truths can only bring the gospel message *unto* our hearts (see 2 Nephi 33:1). Ultimately, we need to act in righteousness and thereby invite the truth *into* our hearts. Only in this way can we, as honest seekers of truth, develop the spiritual capacity to find answers for ourselves and draw closer to Heavenly Father and Jesus Christ.

We progress toward becoming converted unto the Lord (see Alma 23:6–8) as we live the principles we learn (see John 7:17) and feel the Spirit confirm that what we are doing is pleasing to our Father in Heaven. We will learn for ourselves simple gospel doctrine and principles in such a way that we will love the Lord and understand that because of Him and His Atonement, we can always retain a remission of our sins.

A PRINCIPLE OF ACTION

Please consider the definition of faith in the Lord as set forth in the *Lectures on Faith*.

"Faith [in Christ is] the first principle in revealed religion, . . . the foundation of all righteousness, . . . and the principle of action in all intelligent beings."[1]

Receiving the spiritual gift of faith in Christ entails the exercise of our moral agency to act in accordance with His teachings and follow Him, learn His doctrine, keep His commandments, bind ourselves to Him through covenants,[2] trust in His promises, and meekly accept His will and timing in our lives. Abiding in the Savior, walking with Him (see Moses 6:34), and living His doctrine and correct principles are essential because "faith without works is dead" (James 2:20). We are to be "doers of the word, and not hearers only" (James 1:22), "that every man may act in doctrine and principle pertaining to futurity, according to the moral agency which [God has] given unto him" (Doctrine and Covenants 101:78).

We also learn in the *Lectures on Faith* that "faith is not only the principle of action, but of power also, . . . whether in heaven or on earth."[3] Faith in Christ always leads to righteous action (see James 2:14–26; Ether 12:4; Alma 7:24; 26:22), which increases our spiritual power and capacity.

Therefore, faithful disciples of Christ are workers "anxiously engaged in a good cause, and do[ing] many things of their own free will, and bring[ing] to pass much righteousness;

"For the power is in them wherein they are agents unto themselves. And inasmuch as men do good they shall in nowise lose their reward.

"But he that doeth not anything until he is commanded, and receiveth a commandment with doubtful heart, and keepeth it with slothfulness, the same is damned" (Doctrine and Covenants 58:27–29).

Exercising faith in Jesus Christ is *trusting* and placing our confidence in Him as our Savior, on His name, and in His promises and relying upon His merits, mercy, and grace (see 2 Nephi 2:8). We begin to come to know the Savior as we arouse our spiritual faculties and experiment upon His teachings, even until we can give place in our souls for a portion of His words. As our faith in the Lord increases, we trust in Him and have confidence in His power to redeem, heal, and strengthen us.

President Russell M. Nelson has said, "The Lord taught us how to increase our faith by seeking '*learning,* even by study and also by faith' [Doctrine and Covenants 88:118; emphasis added]. We strengthen our faith in Jesus Christ as we strive to keep

His commandments and 'always remember him' [Moroni 4:3]. Further, our faith increases every time we *exercise* our faith in Him. That is what learning by faith means."[4]

Hearing God's word and receiving the spiritual gift of faith in the Savior are closely related, as "faith cometh by hearing, and hearing by the word of God" (Romans 10:17). We become acquainted with Him and His voice as we study and feast upon His word in the scriptures, pray to the Father in His name with real intent, and seek for the constant companionship of the Holy Ghost. Learning and applying in our lives the doctrine of Christ is a prerequisite to receiving the gift of faith in Him.

INTELLIGENCE COMES THROUGH OBEDIENCE

One way we exercise our faith and become "doers of the word" is through obedience, the blessing of which is true intelligence. The revelations teach us that "the glory of God is intelligence" (Doctrine and Covenants 93:36). Now, we typically may think the word *intelligence* in this scripture denotes cognitive ability or a particular gift for academic or other types of work. In this verse, however, one of the meanings of intelligence is the *application* of the knowledge we obtain for righteous purposes.

How we think about many things changes dramatically when we understand that intelligence is applying what we learn and know for righteousness. For example, given this gospel definition, we should not equate intelligence with formal education, performance on standardized examinations, academic degrees, or worldly success. By this standard, some of the most educated people I have ever known have little or no intelligence. And some of the most intelligent people I have ever known have little or no formal education.

This definition of intelligence also helps us to recognize the crucial role of obedience in learning and living the Savior's gospel. Consider the following verses from the Doctrine and Covenants.

"Whatever principle of intelligence we attain unto in this life, it will rise with us in the resurrection.

"And if a person gains more knowledge and intelligence in this life through his diligence and obedience than another, he will have so much the advantage in the world to come" (Doctrine and Covenants 130:18–19).

The order in which knowledge and intelligence are listed in verse 19 is instructive—with *knowledge* first and *intelligence* second. Also, the parallel sequencing between knowledge and intelligence and the means by which they are acquired should be considered:

"And if a person gains more knowledge and intelligence in this life through his *diligence* and *obedience* . . ."

Interestingly, knowledge is associated with diligence. Significantly, intelligence is linked to obedience.

Through persistent, effective, and diligent work, a person can accumulate knowledge in the form of facts, data, information, and experience. Intelligence, however, can be gained only through obedience.

My beloved fellow servants in the work of the Lord, intelligence is faithfully obeying God's commandments and applying the principles of the Savior's gospel in our lives. Obedience is the means whereby we can learn in mortality the things that truly matter the most in eternity.[5]

In this special season of the dispensation of the fulness of times, our heartfelt and willing obedience to God's commandments can help us become the most intelligent people who have ever lived on this planet. Armed with true intelligence and enduring personal testimonies of the gospel, we can receive divine, enabling strength and become more securely anchored to the "rock" of Jesus Christ.

GATHER TOGETHER IN ONE ALL THINGS IN CHRIST– OBTAINING THE GREATEST PERSPECTIVE OF TRUTH

CHAPTER 10

SEGMENTING VERSUS LINKING

Honoring our covenant connection with God and the Savior and obeying the divine commandment to ask, seek, and knock synergistically help us (1) seek for the spiritual gift of faith in the Lord and (2) press forward in building the spiritual foundation of our lives upon Him. Likewise, the important principle of "[gathering] together in one all things in Christ" (Ephesians 1:10) can be applied to all gospel truths, and doing so often yields increased spiritual perspective, greater understanding, and, ultimately, a spiritual foundation more securely anchored to the "rock of our Redeemer" (Helaman 5:12).

While the Lord invites us to gather together in one all things in Him, we may often segment gospel truths in ways that limit our understanding and vision. We may sometimes give undue emphasis to separate categories of the work of salvation and the associated policies and procedures. I fear that many of us may focus so exclusively and intensely on specific facets of the Lord's work that we fail to garner the full power of this comprehensive labor of salvation and exaltation.

When carried to an extreme, priority is given to managing programs and enhancing statistics over inviting individuals to enter into covenants and receive ordinances worthily.

Sometimes as members of the Church we segment, separate, and apply the gospel in our lives by creating lengthy checklists of individual topics to study and tasks to accomplish. We must be careful because pharisaical focus upon checklists can divert us from drawing closer to the Lord.

LEARNING AND LINKING GOSPEL TRUTHS

The principle of *gathering together in one—even in Him*—can assist us in changing the traditional checklists into a unified, integrated, and complete whole and offer a higher perspective of the Lord's work in our lives. Let me provide both a doctrinal and a Church example of what I am suggesting.

Example 1. The fourth article of faith is one of the greatest illustrations of gathering together in one all things in Christ: "We believe that the first principles and ordinances of the Gospel are: first, Faith in the Lord Jesus Christ; second, Repentance; third, Baptism by immersion for the remission of sins; fourth, Laying on of hands for the gift of the Holy Ghost" (Articles of Faith 1:4).

True faith is focused in and on the Lord Jesus Christ—in Him as the divine and Only Begotten Son of the Father and on Him and the redemptive mission He fulfilled. "For he hath answered the ends of the law, and he claimeth all those who have faith in him; and they who have faith in him will cleave unto every good thing; wherefore he advocateth the cause of the children of men" (Moroni 7:28). We exercise faith in Christ as we *trust* and place our confidence in Him as our Savior.

The first and natural consequence of trusting in the Savior is repenting and turning away from evil. As we exercise faith in and on the Lord, we naturally turn toward, come unto, and depend upon Him. Thus, repentance is *trusting* in and *relying* upon the Redeemer to do for us what we cannot do for ourselves. Each of us must "[*rely*] wholly upon the merits of him who is mighty to save" (2 Nephi 31:19; emphasis added) because only "through the merits, and mercy, and grace of the Holy Messiah" (2 Nephi 2:8) can we become new creatures in Christ (see 2 Corinthians 5:17) and ultimately return to and dwell in the presence of God.

The ordinance of baptism by immersion for the remission of sins requires us to *trust* in Him, *rely* upon Him, and *follow* Him. Nephi proclaimed, "I know that if ye shall *follow the Son,* with full purpose of heart, acting no hypocrisy and no deception before God, but with real intent, repenting of your sins, witnessing unto the Father that ye are willing to take upon you the name of Christ, by baptism—yea, by *following your Lord and your Savior* down into the water, according to his word, behold, then shall ye receive the Holy Ghost; yea, then cometh the baptism of fire and of the Holy Ghost" (2 Nephi 31:13; emphasis added).

Next, the ordinance of laying on of hands for the gift of the Holy Ghost requires us to *trust* in Him, *rely* upon Him, *follow* Him, and *press forward* in Him with the assistance of His Holy Spirit. As Nephi declared, "And now . . . I know by this that unless a man shall endure to the end, in following the example of the Son of the living God, he cannot be saved" (2 Nephi 31:16).

The fourth article of faith does not simply identify the fundamental principles and ordinances of the restored gospel. Rather, this inspired statement of beliefs gathers together in one all things in Christ: *trusting* in and on Him, *relying* upon Him, *following* Him, and *pressing forward* with Him—even in Him.

Example 2. I now want to describe how all Church programs and initiatives are gathered together in one in Christ. Many additional illustrations could be presented; I will use only a selected few.

In 1978, President Spencer W. Kimball instructed members of the Church to build up the strength of Zion throughout the world. He counseled the Saints to remain in their native lands and establish strong stakes by gathering the family of God and teaching them the ways of the Lord. He further indicated that more houses of the Lord would be built and promised blessings for the Saints wherever they lived in the world.[1]

As the number of stakes increased, the need was intensified for member homes to "become [places] where family members [loved] to be, where they [could] enrich their lives and find mutual love, support, appreciation, and encouragement."[2] Consequently, in 1980, Sunday meetings were consolidated into a three-hour block to reemphasize "personal and family responsibility for learning, living, and teaching the gospel."[3] This emphasis on family and the home again was affirmed in "The Family: A Proclamation to the World," introduced by President Gordon B. Hinckley in 1995.[4]

In April of 1998, President Hinckley announced the construction of many more houses of the Lord, thereby bringing the sacred ordinances of the temple closer to Latter-day Saint individuals and families throughout the world.[5] And these enhanced opportunities for spiritual growth and development were complemented by related increases in temporal self-reliance through the introduction of the Perpetual Education Fund in 2001.[6]

During his administration, President Thomas S. Monson repeatedly exhorted the Saints to go "to the rescue" and emphasized caring for the poor and needy as one of the Church's divinely appointed responsibilities. Continuing the emphasis on temporal preparation, the Self-Reliance Services initiative was implemented in 2012.

Over the past several years, essential principles about making the Sabbath day a delight in the home and at church have been emphasized and reinforced,[7] thus preparing us for the 2018 adjustment of the Sunday meeting schedule to a two-hour block.

Melchizedek Priesthood quorums were strengthened and aligned more effectively with Church organizations to accomplish a higher and holier approach to ministering.

I believe that the sequence and timing of these actions over many decades can help us to see one united and comprehensive work and not just a series of independent and discrete initiatives. "God has revealed a pattern of spiritual progress for individuals and families through ordinances, teaching, programs, and activities that are *home centered and Church supported.* Church organizations and programs exist to bless individuals and families and are not ends in themselves."[8]

All of these interrelated actions are part of a unified effort to better align the focus, resources, and work of the Savior's restored Church with its fundamental mission: to assist God in His work to bring to pass the salvation and exaltation of His children.

I pray we can recognize the Lord's work as one great worldwide work that is becoming ever more home centered and Church supported. I know and testify that the Lord is revealing and "will yet reveal many great and important things pertaining to the Kingdom of God" (Articles of Faith 1:9).

Increased perspective, purpose, and power will be evident in our learning and living of the restored gospel of Jesus Christ as we strive to gather together in one all things in Christ. In the following chapters we will consider other examples of how this principle applies in practical ways to learning and living His restored gospel in our daily lives.

CHAPTER 11

A MORE COMPLETE AND CORRECT UNDERSTANDING

Following the counsel to "gather together in one all things in Christ" (Ephesians 1:10) aids our efforts to learn and teach correct principles and makes our understanding of foundational and eternal truths more complete. The Lord revealed to the Prophet Joseph Smith that "the elders, priests and teachers of this church shall teach the principles of my gospel, which are in the Bible and the Book of Mormon, in the which is the fulness of the gospel" (Doctrine and Covenants 42:12). He also declared that the Latter-day Saints should "be instructed more perfectly in theory, in principle, in doctrine, in the law of the gospel, in all things that pertain unto the kingdom of God, that are expedient for you to understand" (Doctrine and Covenants 88:78).

When Joseph Smith was imprisoned in Liberty Jail, he wrote letters of instruction to Church members and leaders and reminded them that "a very large ship is benefited very much by a very small helm in the time of a storm, by being kept workways with the wind and the waves" (Doctrine and Covenants 123:16).

A "helm" is a wheel or tiller and the associated equipment used to steer a ship or a boat. And "workways with the wind and the waves" denotes turning a ship so that it maintains its balance and does not capsize during a storm.

Gospel principles are for me and you what a helm is to a ship. Stated succinctly, a gospel principle is a doctrinally based guideline for the righteous exercise of moral agency. Principles derive from broader gospel truths and provide direction and standards as we press forward on the covenant path.

For example, the first three articles of faith identify fundamental aspects of the doctrine of the restored gospel of Jesus Christ: the nature of the Godhead in the first article of faith, the effects of the Fall of Adam and Eve in the second article of faith, and the blessings made possible through the Atonement of Jesus Christ in the third article of faith (see Articles of Faith 1:1–3). And the fourth article of faith sets forth the first principles—the guidelines of exercising faith in Jesus Christ and repenting—and the first priesthood ordinances that enable the Atonement of Jesus Christ to be efficacious in our lives (see Articles of Faith 1:4).

THE PLAN OF REDEMPTION AND OBEDIENCE TO GOD'S COMMANDMENTS

The relationship between Heavenly Father's great plan of redemption and obedience to the commandments is a prime example of the interrelatedness of gospel truths. Although obedience frequently is described as the first law of heaven, each of us should always remember that this foundational law does not stand independent and alone. Rather, it is connected with and central to all gospel truths and principles.

I have observed and learned that the essential and eternal importance of the law of obedience is best understood within the context of Heavenly Father's plan of happiness and the atoning sacrifice of the Lord Jesus Christ. This basic truth is illustrated powerfully in the Book of Mormon as Alma testifies to Zeezrom. The account features a mighty missionary teaching an antagonistic lawyer about mortal life as a probationary state and how the plan of redemption brings to pass the Resurrection and, through faith in Jesus Christ and repentance, a remission of sins.

"Wherefore, he gave commandments unto men, they having first transgressed the first commandments as to things which were temporal, and becoming as gods, knowing good from evil, placing themselves in a state to act, or being placed in a state to act according to their wills and pleasures, whether to do evil or to do good—

"Therefore God gave unto them commandments, after having made known unto them the plan of redemption, that they should not do evil" (Alma 12:31–32).

Alma's instruction highlights an essential relationship between *the plan of redemption* and *obedience to God's commandments.* Notice that Alma emphasized the role of commandments within the doctrinal context of the plan. All of us need to follow his instructive example in our work of teaching and testifying.

"Gathering" these two gospel principles together leads to a more complete and correct understanding, and correct principles enable us to find our way and to stand firm, steadfast, and immovable so we do not lose our balance and fall in the raging latter-day storms of darkness and confusion.

BAPTISM, CONFIRMATION, AND THE SACRAMENT

I now want to describe briefly how segmenting doctrine can sometimes hinder understanding. Though perhaps well-intentioned, seemingly slight deviations from fundamental gospel doctrine and principles can impact individuals and families across generations.

I invite you to answer a few simple questions in your mind and heart.

First question: At some time in your life, have you ever wished you could be baptized again?

I believe that if we are honest with ourselves, all or almost all of us surely have yearned for such a second spiritual start in our lives and to be as clean and worthy as the day on which we received our first saving gospel ordinances.

Second question: Why might we believe a second baptism

could be the principal source of a second spiritual start in our lives?

Third question: Are children who are preparing for baptism equally eager to be confirmed members of The Church of Jesus Christ of Latter-day Saints and receive the gift of the Holy Ghost as they are to be baptized? If not, why?

Fourth question: Are children who are preparing for baptism as eager to participate in the ordinance of the sacrament on the Sunday following their baptismal service as they are to be baptized? If not, why?

I respectfully suggest that in many instances we typically give far greater emphasis to the ordinance of baptism and, as the Primary song suggests, having "[our] wrongs . . . washed away"[1] than we give to the ordinances of confirmation, receiving the gift of the Holy Ghost, and the sacrament. Consequently, this imbalance and an incomplete or inaccurate understanding of foundational gospel doctrine and principles may cause Church members to yearn for a second opportunity to be baptized.

Please understand that I am not suggesting anyone is intentionally doing anything wrong, and I am not suggesting we should give less emphasis to the baptismal ordinance. I am suggesting that some aspects of our Church culture and traditions may blind us to the unintended consequences of seemingly innocent but incorrect beliefs and practices.

I am suggesting that one way we can gather together in one

all things in Christ is by giving more unified and comprehensive emphasis to the baptismal ordinance, the laying on of hands for the gift of the Holy Ghost, the sanctifying and purifying power of the Spirit, and the ordinance of the sacrament.

Baptism by immersion for the remission of sins "is the introductory ordinance of the gospel"[2] of Jesus Christ and must be preceded by faith in the Savior and by sincere repentance. This ordinance "is a sign and a commandment which God has set for [His children] to enter into His kingdom."[3]

The baptismal covenant includes fundamental commitments: (1) to be willing to take upon ourselves the name of Jesus Christ, (2) to always remember and serve Him, and (3) to keep His commandments. The promised blessing for honoring this covenant is "that [we] may always have his Spirit to be with [us]" (Doctrine and Covenants 20:77; see also Doctrine and Covenants 20:79; Mosiah 18:10). Thus, baptism is the essential preparation to receive the authorized opportunity for the constant companionship of the third member of the Godhead.

Baptism by water "must be followed by baptism of the Spirit in order to be complete."[4] As the Savior taught Nicodemus, "Except a man be born of water and of the Spirit, he cannot enter into the kingdom of God" (John 3:5).

Three statements by the Prophet Joseph Smith emphasize the vital linkage between the ordinances of baptism by immersion for the remission of sins and the laying on of hands for the gift of the Holy Ghost.

Statement 1: "Baptism is a holy ordinance preparatory to the reception of the Holy Ghost; it is the channel and key by which the Holy Ghost will be administered."[5]

Statement 2: "You might as well baptize a bag of sand as a man, if not done in view of the remission of sins and getting of the Holy Ghost. Baptism by water is but half a baptism, and is good for nothing without the other half—that is, the baptism of the Holy Ghost."[6]

Statement 3: "The baptism of water, without the baptism of fire and the Holy Ghost attending it, is of no use. They are necessarily and inseparably connected."[7]

The consistent connectedness of the principle of repentance, the ordinances of baptism and receiving the gift of the Holy Ghost, and the glorious blessing of an ongoing remission of sins is emphasized repeatedly in the scriptures. We are not cleansed from sin by the single act of being immersed in water.

Nephi declared, "For the gate by which ye should enter is repentance and baptism by water; *and then cometh a remission of your sins by fire and by the Holy Ghost*" (2 Nephi 31:17; emphasis added).

The Savior Himself proclaimed, "Now this is the commandment: Repent, all ye ends of the earth, and come unto me and be baptized in my name, *that ye may be sanctified by the reception of the Holy Ghost,* that ye may stand spotless before me at the last day" (3 Nephi 27:20; emphasis added).

The ordinance of confirming a new member of the Church and bestowing the gift of the Holy Ghost is both simple and profound. Worthy Melchizedek Priesthood holders place their hands upon the head of an individual and call him or her by name. Then, by the authority of the holy priesthood and in the name of the Savior, the individual is confirmed a member of The Church of Jesus Christ of Latter-day Saints, and this important phrase is uttered: "Receive the Holy Ghost."

These four words—"receive the Holy Ghost"—are not a passive pronouncement; rather, they constitute a priesthood injunction—an authoritative admonition to act and not simply to be acted upon (see 2 Nephi 2:26). The Holy Ghost does not become operative in our lives merely because hands are placed upon our heads and those four important words are spoken. As we receive this ordinance, each of us accepts a sacred and ongoing responsibility to desire, to seek, to work, and to so live that we indeed "receive the Holy Ghost" and the attendant spiritual gifts. "For what doth it profit a man if a gift is bestowed upon him, and he receive not the gift? Behold, he rejoices not in that which is given unto him, neither rejoices in him who is the giver of the gift" (Doctrine and Covenants 88:33).

In the process of coming unto the Savior and pressing forward along the covenant path, receiving the sanctifying power of the

Holy Ghost in our lives creates the possibility of an *ongoing cleansing* of our soul from sin. This joyous blessing is essential because "no unclean thing can dwell with God" (1 Nephi 10:21).

The ordinance of the sacrament is a holy and repeated invitation to repent sincerely and to be renewed spiritually. The act of partaking of the sacramental emblems, in and of itself, does not remit sins. But as we prepare conscientiously and participate in this holy ordinance with a broken heart and a contrite spirit, then the promise is that we may *always* have the Spirit of the Lord to be with us. And by the sanctifying power of the Holy Ghost as our constant companion, we can *always* retain a remission of our sins. Thus, the gospel of Jesus Christ provides second and third and fourth and endless opportunities to retain a remission of our sins.

If candidates for baptism, young or old, learn about and understand for themselves the interrelationship among baptism, receiving the gift of the Holy Ghost, and the ordinance of the sacrament, would any of them ever have the desire to be baptized a second time?

Our Heavenly Father and His Beloved Son do not intend for us to experience a feeling of spiritual renewal, refreshment, and restoration just once in our lives, when we are baptized. The blessings of obtaining and always retaining a remission of our sins through gospel ordinances help us understand that baptism is a point of departure in our mortal spiritual journey; it is not a destination we should yearn to revisit over and over again.

By gathering these seemingly separate truths together in Christ, our understanding becomes clearer and our faith in eternal truths is strengthened. Imagine a generation of converts and eight-year-old children with the doctrine of Christ written in the fleshy tables of their hearts so completely and deeply that they would never even think the thought about being baptized a second time. And contemplate family members, friends, and young children even more eager to participate in the ordinance of the sacrament on the Sunday following their baptismal service than they were to be baptized. Surely such individuals would stand on strong spiritual foundations and be blessed with firmness of heart, mind, might, and strength.

CHAPTER 12

ONE GREAT WORK

————◆————

I present here one more, lengthier example of how gathering "together in one all things in Christ" (Ephesians 1:10) leads to greater understanding and a richer perspective. Let us consider the interrelatedness of missionary work and the work of redeeming our deceased ancestors. These two sacred, divinely appointed responsibilities are often segmented, studied, and enacted separately, yet when we gather them together, we see clearly that they are part of the same marvelous work of salvation and exaltation in the dispensation of the fulness of times.

MORONI'S FIRST VISIT TO JOSEPH SMITH

Approximately three years after the First Vision, on the night of September 21, 1823, young Joseph Smith was praying to receive a remission of his sins and to know of his state and standing before God (see Joseph Smith—History 1:29). A personage appeared at his bedside, called Joseph by name, and declared "he was a messenger sent from the presence of God . . . and that his name was Moroni." He explained "that God had a work for [Joseph] to do" (Joseph Smith—History 1:33) and then instructed him about the coming forth of the Book of Mormon. Significantly, the Book of Mormon was one of the first topics addressed in Moroni's message.

The Book of Mormon is another testament of Jesus Christ and the great tool of conversion in the latter days. Our purpose in sharing the gospel is to invite all to come unto Jesus Christ (see Moroni 10:30–33), receive the blessings of the restored gospel, and endure to the end through faith in the Savior.[1] Helping individuals to experience the mighty change of heart (see Alma 5:12–14) and bind themselves to Heavenly Father and His Son through sacred covenants and ordinances is the fundamental objective of preaching the gospel.

Moroni's introduction of the Book of Mormon to Joseph Smith initiated the work of salvation and exaltation for individuals on *this side of the veil* in the dispensation of the fulness of times.

Continuing his instruction to Joseph, Moroni next quoted from the book of Malachi in the Old Testament, with a little variation from the language used in the King James Version:

"Behold, I will reveal unto you the Priesthood, by the hand

of Elijah the prophet, before the coming of the great and dreadful day of the Lord.

". . . And he shall plant in the hearts of the children the promises made to the fathers, and the hearts of the children shall turn to their fathers. If it were not so, the whole earth would be utterly wasted at his coming" (Joseph Smith—History 1:38–39).

Our purpose in building houses of the Lord is to make available the holy places wherein the sacred covenants and ordinances necessary for the salvation and exaltation of the human family can be administered, for both the living and the dead. Moroni's instruction to Joseph Smith about the vital role of Elijah and priesthood authority expanded the work of salvation and exaltation on *this side of the veil* and initiated in our dispensation the work for the dead on *the other side of the veil.*

In summary, Moroni's teachings in September of 1823 about the Book of Mormon and the mission of Elijah established the doctrinal foundation for the work of salvation and exaltation on *both sides of the veil.*

TEACHINGS OF THE PROPHET JOSEPH SMITH

The lessons Joseph Smith learned from Moroni influenced every aspect of his ministry. For example, at a solemn assembly held in the Kirtland Temple on April 6, 1837, the Prophet Joseph Smith spoke on matters pertaining to the priesthood and priesthood quorums. He explained to the assembled brethren: "After all that has been said, the greatest and most important duty is to preach the Gospel."[2]

Almost precisely seven years later, on April 7, 1844, Joseph Smith delivered a sermon now known as the King Follet Discourse. In that address the Prophet Joseph Smith declared, "The greatest responsibility in this world that God has laid upon us is to seek after our dead. The Apostle says, 'They without us cannot be made perfect' [Doctrine and Covenants 128:15]; for it is necessary that the sealing power should be in our hands to seal our children and our dead for the fulness of the dispensation of times—a dispensation to meet the promises made by Jesus Christ before the foundation of the world for the salvation of man."[3]

Some individuals may wonder how both preaching the gospel *and* seeking after our dead can be simultaneously the greatest duties and responsibilities God has placed upon His children. I believe the Prophet Joseph Smith was emphasizing in both statements the fundamental truth that covenants, entered into through authoritative priesthood ordinances, can bind us to Heavenly Father and the Lord Jesus Christ and are the essential core of the work of salvation and exaltation on both sides of the veil. I suggest that these teachings highlight the unity and oneness of the latter-day work of salvation.

Our missionary responsibilities and family history and temple work are complementary and interrelated aspects of one great work, "that in the dispensation of the fulness of times he might gather together in one all things in Christ, both which are in heaven, and which are on earth; even in him" (Ephesians 1:10). Thus, the two statements by the Prophet that initially may appear contradictory, in fact, highlight the focal point of this great latter-day work.

HEARTS, COVENANTS, AND PRIESTHOOD ORDINANCES

Preaching the gospel and seeking after our dead are two divinely appointed responsibilities that relate to both our hearts and priesthood ordinances. The essence of the Lord's work is changing, turning, and purifying hearts through covenants and ordinances performed by proper priesthood authority.

The word *heart* is used over one thousand times in the standard works and symbolizes the inner feelings of an individual. Thus, our hearts—the sum total of our desires, affections, intentions, motives, and attitudes—define who we are and determine what we will become.

The Lord's purpose for missionary work is to invite all to come unto Christ, receive the blessings of the restored gospel, and endure to the end through faith in Christ.[4] We do not share the gospel merely to increase the numerical size and strength of the latter-day Church. Rather, we seek to fulfill the divinely appointed responsibility to proclaim the reality of the Father's plan of happiness, the divinity of His Only Begotten Son, Jesus Christ, and the efficacy of the Savior's atoning sacrifice. Inviting all to "come unto

Christ" (Moroni 10:30–33), experiencing the "mighty change of heart" (Alma 5:12–14), and offering the ordinances of salvation to individuals in mortality not yet under covenant are the fundamental objectives of preaching the gospel.

Enabling the exaltation of the living and the dead is the purpose for building houses of the Lord and performing vicarious ordinances. We do not worship in holy temples solely to have a memorable individual or family experience. Rather, we seek to fulfill the divinely appointed responsibility to offer the ordinances of salvation and exaltation to the entire human family. Planting in the hearts of the children the promises made to the fathers—even Abraham, Isaac, and Jacob; turning the hearts of the children to their own fathers; and performing family history research and vicarious ordinances in the temple are labors that bless individuals in the spirit world not yet under covenant.

Priesthood ordinances are the pathway to the power of godliness: "And this greater priesthood administereth the gospel and holdeth the key of the mysteries of the kingdom, even the key of the knowledge of God. Therefore, in the ordinances thereof, the power of godliness is manifest. And without the ordinances thereof, and the authority of the priesthood, the power of godliness is not manifest unto men in the flesh" (Doctrine and Covenants 84:19–21).

Please consider the sobering significance of these verses. An individual *must* first pass through the gate of baptism and receive the gift of the Holy Ghost—and then continue to press forward along the path of covenants and ordinances that leads to the Savior and the blessings of His Atonement (see 2 Nephi 31). Priesthood ordinances are essential to fully "come unto Christ, and be perfected in Him" (Moroni 10:32). Without the ordinances, an individual cannot receive all of the blessings made possible through the Lord's infinite and eternal atoning sacrifice (see Alma 34:10–14)—even the power of godliness.

The Lord's work is one majestic labor focused upon hearts, covenants, and priesthood ordinances.

CHANGING AND TURNING HEARTS

This divine doctrine suggests an important implication for our work in the Church: although in our study and teaching we often separate temple and family history work from the work of proclaiming the gospel, in reality, both are central in and vital to the work of salvation. Perhaps the Lord was emphasizing this truth in the very sequence of events that occurred as the fulness of the gospel was restored to the earth in these latter days.

In the sacred grove, Joseph Smith saw and talked with the Eternal Father and Jesus Christ. This vision ushered in the "dispensation of the fulness of times" (Ephesians 1:10) and enabled Joseph to learn about the true nature of the Godhead and of continual revelation.

About three years later, in response to earnest prayer on the evening of September 21, 1823, Joseph's bedroom filled with light until it was "lighter than at noonday" (Joseph Smith—History 1:30). The angel Moroni appeared and taught Joseph about the coming forth of the Book of Mormon. And then Moroni quoted from the book of Malachi: "Behold, I will reveal unto you the Priesthood, by the hand of Elijah the prophet, before the coming of the great and dreadful day of the Lord.

". . . And he shall plant in the hearts of the children the promises made to the fathers, and the hearts of the children shall turn to their fathers. If it were not so, the whole earth would be utterly wasted at his coming" (Joseph Smith—History 1:38–39).

Moroni's instructions to the young prophet ultimately included two primary themes: (1) the Book of Mormon and (2) the words of Malachi foretelling the role of Elijah in the restoration "of all things, which God hath spoken by the mouth of all his holy prophets since the world began" (Acts 3:21). Thus, the introductory events of the Restoration revealed a correct understanding of the Godhead, established the reality of continuing revelation, emphasized the importance of the Book of Mormon, and anticipated the work of salvation and exaltation for both the living and the dead.

Please now consider the role of the Book of Mormon in changing hearts—and of temple and family history work in turning hearts.

The Book of Mormon in combination with the Spirit of the

Lord is the greatest single tool God has given us to convert the world.[5] This Restoration volume of scripture is the keystone of our religion and is essential in bringing souls to the Savior. The Book of Mormon is another testament of Jesus Christ—a vital confirming witness of the divinity of the Redeemer in a world that grows ever more secular and cynical. Hearts are changed as individuals read and study the Book of Mormon and pray with real intent to learn of the truthfulness of the book.

The spirit of Elijah is "a manifestation of the Holy Ghost bearing witness of the divine nature of the family."[6] This distinctive influence of the Holy Ghost bears powerful witness of the Father's plan of happiness and draws people to search out and cherish their ancestors and family members—both past and present. The spirit of Elijah affects people both inside and outside of the Church and causes hearts to turn to the fathers.

The time has come for us to capitalize more effectively on the potent combination of the mighty change of heart, made possible primarily by the spiritual power of the Book of Mormon, and the turning of hearts to the fathers, accomplished through temple and family history work. A yearning for connection to our past can prepare an individual to receive the virtue of the word of God and fortify his or her faith. A heart turning to the fathers uniquely helps an individual withstand the influence of the adversary and strengthen conversion.

The Lord has inspired technologies and tools that enable us

to benefit from the oneness of proclaiming the gospel and temple and family history work more than at any previous time in this dispensation. It is no coincidence that these innovations have come forth at precisely the time they are so needed to advance missionary work all over the earth. The Lord's work is one majestic effort focused upon hearts that change and turn, on sacred covenants, and upon the power of godliness manifested through priesthood ordinances.

The Lord declared, "I am able to do mine own work" (2 Nephi 27:21) and "I will hasten my work in its time" (Doctrine and Covenants 88:73). We are witnesses of His hastening of His work.

We live and serve in the dispensation of the fulness of times. Recognizing the eternal importance of the distinctive dispensation in which we live should influence all that we do and strive to become. The work of salvation to be accomplished in these last days is grand, vast, essential, and urgent. How grateful each of us should be for the blessings and responsibilities of living in this specific season of the final dispensation. How humble we should be knowing that "unto whom much is given much is required" (Doctrine and Covenants 82:3).

Preaching the gospel and seeking after our dead are complementary parts of one great work—a labor of love intended to change, turn, and purify the hearts of honest seekers of truth. The artificial boundary line we so often place between missionary efforts and temple and family history work is being erased; this is one great work of salvation.[7]

Can we begin to understand the role of temple and family history work in helping us obtain a deeper understanding of the plan of salvation? Do we recognize that one of the greatest influences on maintaining our participation in the gospel is the Holy Ghost bearing witness to us of the divine nature of the family? Can we more fully appreciate the importance of heart-turning moments occasioned by the sharing of family stories? Do we see that we can access more often the powers of godliness by participating worthily in ordinances such as the sacrament and baptisms and confirmations for the dead?

By gathering missionary work and temple and family history work together, we are enabled to see clearly, hear unmistakably, and ever remember the importance of our service in the Lord's work of changing, turning, and purifying hearts.

COME UNTO CHRIST
AND FEAR NOT

To face the future with faith, hope, and power, our lives need to be anchored to the "rock of our Redeemer" (Helaman 5:12). We are connected securely to and with Heavenly Father and the Savior as we worthily receive ordinances and enter into covenants, faithfully remember and honor those sacred commitments, and do our best to live in accordance with the covenant conditions we have accepted. And as we accept the invitation to ask, seek, and knock for the spiritual gift of faith in Christ and strive to learn for ourselves eternal truths, we further strengthen our bond to God and the Savior. And it is through that bond that we receive spiritual strength and stability.

President Russell M. Nelson has repeatedly emphasized the need for each of us to have a firm spiritual foundation. "Just as the physical foundation of the Salt Lake Temple must be strong enough to withstand natural disasters, our *spiritual* foundations must be solid. Then, when metaphorical earthquakes rock our lives, we can stand 'steadfast and immovable' [Mosiah 5:15] because of our faith [in Jesus Christ]."[1]

Elder Neil L. Andersen summarized well how to develop a solid spiritual foundation and the blessings that we will receive as a result. He said, "Don't let the whirlwinds drag you down. These are your days—to stand strong as disciples of the Lord Jesus Christ [see Helaman 7:9].

"Build more firmly your foundation upon the rock of your Redeemer.

"Treasure more completely His incomparable life and teachings.

"Follow more diligently His example and His commandments.

"Embrace more deeply His love, His mercy and grace, and the powerful gifts of His Atonement.

"As you do, I promise you that you will see the whirlwinds for what they are—tests, temptations, distractions, or challenges to help you grow. And as you live righteously year after year, I assure you that your experiences will confirm to you again and again that Jesus is the Christ. The spiritual rock under your feet will be solid and secure. You will rejoice that God has placed you here to be a part of the final preparations for Christ's glorious return."[2]

HUSH OUR FEARS

Many blessings come from building our spiritual foundation upon the rock of our Redeemer—blessings of purpose, power, knowledge, strength, and perspective. Additionally, we can receive the blessings of confidence and peace. Even when facing the confusion and adversity so common in the latter days, the Lord can help us hush our fears. We can be blessed through the power of the Holy Ghost to "be still" (Psalm 46:10)—to have a personal, spiritual assurance that God is our Heavenly Father, we are His children, and Jesus Christ is our Savior.

I remember vividly an experience I had as a small boy. One day while playing with my friends, I accidentally broke a window in a store near our home. As the glass shattered and the security alarm blared, a paralyzing fear filled my heart and mind. I realized immediately I was doomed to spend the remainder of my life in prison. My parents eventually coaxed me out from a hiding place under my bed and helped me to make amends with the store owner. Fortunately, my jail sentence was commuted.

The fear I felt that day was overwhelming and real. You undoubtedly have experienced much greater feelings of dread after learning about a personal health challenge, discovering a family member in difficulty or danger, or observing disturbing world events. In such instances, the distressing emotion of fear arises because of impending danger, uncertainty, or pain and through experiences that are unexpected, sometimes sudden, and likely to produce a negative outcome.

In our daily lives, endless reports of criminal violence, famine, wars, corruption, terrorism, declining values, disease, and the destructive forces of nature can engender fear and apprehension. Surely we live in the season foretold by the Lord: "And in that day . . . the whole earth shall be in commotion, and men's hearts shall fail them" (Doctrine and Covenants 45:26).

Fear is dispelled as we anchor our lives to the rock of our Redeemer through a correct knowledge of and faith in the Lord Jesus Christ, as well as through our covenant connection to Him and Heavenly Father.

Speaking of the strengthening renovations then being made to the Salt Lake Temple, President Russell M. Nelson said that "there will be *no safer* place during an earthquake in the Salt Lake Valley than inside that temple.

"Likewise, whenever any kind of upheaval occurs in your life, the safest place to be *spiritually* is living *inside* your temple covenants!

"Please believe me when I say that when your spiritual foundation is built solidly upon Jesus Christ, you have *no need to fear.* As you are true to your covenants made in the temple, you will be strengthened by His power. Then, when spiritual earthquakes occur, you will be able to stand *strong* because your spiritual foundation is solid and immovable."[3]

MORTAL FEAR

Upon hearing the voice of God after partaking of the forbidden fruit, Adam and Eve hid themselves in the Garden of Eden.

God called unto Adam and asked, "Where art thou? And [Adam answered], I heard thy voice . . . , and I was afraid" (Genesis 3:9–10). Notably, one of the first effects of the Fall was for Adam and Eve to experience fear. This potent emotion is an important element of our mortal existence.

An example from the Book of Mormon highlights the power of the knowledge of the Lord (see 2 Peter 1:2–8; Alma 23:5–6) to dispel fear and provide peace even as we confront great adversity.

In the land of Helam, Alma's people were frightened by an advancing Lamanite army.

"But Alma went forth and stood among them, and exhorted them that they should not be frightened, but . . . should remember the Lord their God and he would deliver them.

"Therefore they hushed their fears" (Mosiah 23:27–28).

Notice Alma did not hush the people's fears. Rather, Alma counseled the believers to remember the Lord and the deliverance only He could bestow (see 2 Nephi 2:8). And knowledge of the Savior's protecting watchcare enabled the people to calm their own fears.

Correct knowledge of and faith in the Lord empower us to quiet our fears because Jesus Christ is the only source of enduring peace. He declared, "Learn of me, and listen to my words; walk in the meekness of my Spirit, and you shall have peace in me" (Doctrine and Covenants 19:23).

The Master also explained, "He who doeth the works of

righteousness shall receive his reward, even peace in this world, and eternal life in the world to come" (Doctrine and Covenants 59:23).

Trust and confidence in Christ and a ready reliance on His merits, mercy, and grace lead to hope, through His Atonement, in the Resurrection and eternal life (see 2 Nephi 2:8; Moroni 7:41). Such faith and hope invite into our lives the sweet peace of conscience for which we all yearn. The power of Jesus Christ's Atonement makes repentance possible and quells the despair caused by sin; it also strengthens us to see, do, and become good in ways that we could never recognize or accomplish with our limited mortal capacity. Truly, one of the great blessings of devoted discipleship is "the peace of God, which passeth all understanding" (Philippians 4:7).

The peace Christ gives allows us to view mortality through the precious perspective of eternity and supplies a spiritual settledness (see Colossians 1:23) that helps us maintain a consistent focus on our heavenly destination. Thus, we can be blessed to hush our fears because His doctrine provides purpose and direction in all aspects of our lives. His ordinances and covenants fortify and comfort in times both good and bad. And His priesthood authority gives assurance that the things that matter most can endure both in time and in eternity.

But can we quiet the fears that so easily and frequently beset us in our contemporary world? The answer to this question is an unequivocal yes. To receive this blessing in our lives, we can look to Christ and press forward with faith in Him—as we do so, we help secure our spiritual foundations to Him, our Redeemer.

LOOK TO CHRIST

The counsel Alma gave to his son Helaman applies precisely to each of us today: "Yea, see that ye look to God and live" (Alma 37:47). We should look to and have our focus firmly fixed upon the Savior at all times and in all places.

Recall how the Lord's Apostles were in a ship, tossed in the midst of the sea. Jesus went to them, walking on the water; but not recognizing Him, they cried out in fear.

"Jesus spake unto them, saying, Be of good cheer; it is I; be not afraid.

"And Peter answered him and said, Lord, if it be thou, bid me come unto thee on the water.

"And he said, Come" (Matthew 14:27–29).

Peter then walked on the water to Jesus.

"But when he saw the wind boisterous, he was afraid," began to sink, and cried out, "Lord, save me.

"And immediately Jesus stretched forth his hand, and caught him, and said unto him, O thou of little faith, wherefore didst thou doubt?" (Matthew 14:30–31).

I envision Peter responding fervently and immediately to the Savior's invitation. With his eyes fixed upon Jesus, he stepped out of the boat and miraculously walked on the water. Only when his gaze was diverted by the wind and the waves did he become afraid and begin to sink.

We can be blessed to conquer our fears and strengthen our faith as we follow the Lord's instruction: "Look unto me in every thought; doubt not, fear not" (Doctrine and Covenants 6:36).

PRESS FORWARD WITH FAITH IN CHRIST

Nephi declared: "Wherefore, ye must press forward with a steadfastness in Christ, having a perfect brightness of hope, and a love of God and of all men. Wherefore, if ye shall press forward, feasting upon the word of Christ, and endure to the end, behold, thus saith the Father: Ye shall have eternal life" (2 Nephi 31:20).

The disciplined endurance described in this verse is the result of spiritual understanding and vision, persistence, patience, and God's grace. Exercising faith in and on the holy name of Jesus Christ, meekly submitting to His will and timing in our lives, and humbly acknowledging His hand in all things yield the peaceable things of the kingdom of God that bring joy and eternal life (see Doctrine and Covenants 42:61). Even as we encounter difficulties and face the uncertainties of the future, we can cheerfully persevere and live a "peaceable life in all godliness and honesty" (1 Timothy 2:2).

We can be blessed to hush our fears as we receive the fortitude that comes from learning and living gospel principles and resolutely pressing forward on the covenant pathway.

THE FEAR OF THE LORD

Different from but related to the fears we often experience is what the scriptures describe as "godly fear" (Hebrews 12:28) or "the fear of the Lord" (Job 28:28; Proverbs 16:6; Isaiah 11:2–3). Unlike worldly fear that creates alarm and anxiety, godly fear is a source of peace, assurance, and confidence.

But how can anything associated with fear be edifying or spiritually helpful?

The righteous fear I am attempting to describe encompasses a deep feeling of reverence, respect, and awe for the Lord Jesus Christ (see Psalms 33:8; 96:4), obedience to His commandments (see Deuteronomy 5:29; 8:6; 10:12; 13:4; Psalm 112:1), and anticipation of the Final Judgment and justice at His hand. Thus, godly fear grows out of a correct understanding of the divine nature and mission of the Lord Jesus Christ, a willingness to submit our will to His will, and a knowledge that every man and woman will be accountable for his or her own sins in the Day of Judgment (see Doctrine and Covenants 101:78; Articles of Faith 1:2).

As the scriptures certify, godly fear "is the beginning of knowledge" (Proverbs 1:7), "the instruction of wisdom" (Proverbs 15:33), a "strong confidence" (Proverbs 14:26), and "a fountain of life" (Proverbs 14:27).

Godly fear dispels mortal fears. It even subdues the haunting concern that we never can be good enough spiritually and never will measure up to the Lord's requirements and expectations. In truth, we cannot be good enough or measure up relying solely upon our own capacity and performance. Our works and desires alone do not and cannot save us. "After all we can do" (2 Nephi 25:23), we are made whole only through the mercy and grace available through the Savior's infinite and eternal atoning sacrifice (see Alma 34:10, 14). Certainly, "we believe that through the Atonement of Christ, all mankind may be saved, by obedience to the laws and ordinances of the gospel" (Articles of Faith 1:3).

Godly fear is loving and trusting in Him. As we fear God more completely, we love Him more perfectly. And "perfect love casteth out all fear" (Moroni 8:16). I promise the bright light of godly fear will chase away the dark shadows of mortal fears (see Doctrine and Covenants 50:25) as we look to the Savior, press forward on His covenant path with consecrated commitment, and build the foundations of our lives upon Him.

I love and revere the Lord. His power and peace are real. He is our Redeemer, and I witness that He lives. And because of Him, our hearts need not be troubled or afraid (see John 14:27), and we will be blessed to hush our fears.

APOSTOLIC WITNESS

I am asked frequently what it means to be a special witness of the name of Jesus Christ in all the world. Sometimes I begin my answer to this question by referring to an experience I had many years ago in a priesthood leadership meeting at which then–Elder James E. Faust of the Quorum of the Twelve Apostles was the presiding authority.

Elder Faust taught us about various ways of knowing the eternal truths that come from God. He then indicated he had received the spiritual witness that qualified him to serve as an ordained special witness long before he was called to the Twelve. I found his teaching both instructive and inspiring.

Elder Faust further explained that the testimony of truth which comes into our souls by the power of the Holy Ghost produces a spiritual knowledge, an illumination, and a conviction more sure, more powerful, and more enduring than can be received through

seeing, hearing, and touching. I always will remember his powerful testimony of the Eternal Father, of a living Savior, and of the
reality of the Restoration—a testimony he indicated was obtained
independent of any other person and in a way that transcended the
five physical senses.

Elder Faust's instruction caused me to reflect on the counsel
of the Savior to His Apostles immediately before His Ascension:

"But ye shall receive power, *after* that the Holy Ghost is come
upon you: and ye shall be witnesses unto me both in Jerusalem,
and in all Judea, and in Samaria, and unto the uttermost part of
the earth" (Acts 1:8; emphasis added).

I also recalled that an angel had appeared to Alma the Younger
and commanded him to cease his evil doings. Alma saw an angel
and heard a voice that shook the earth (see Mosiah 27:14–15).
Yet, in bearing testimony of the Savior's doctrine to the people of
Zarahemla, Alma made no mention of these miraculous physical
manifestations.

"Behold, I testify unto you that I do know that these things
whereof I have spoken are true. . . .

"They are made known unto me by the Holy Spirit of God.
. . . And now I do know *of myself* that they are true; for the Lord
God hath made them manifest unto me by his Holy Spirit; and
this is the spirit of revelation which is in me" (Alma 5:45–46;
emphasis added).

Today I understand more completely what Elder Faust was

teaching us in that leadership meeting. I likewise received the spiritual witness that enables me to serve as a special witness of the name of Christ in all the world long before I was ordained and set apart as one of the Twelve Apostles. Certainly my testimony has grown and become stronger and deeper through personal, sacred, and sweet spiritual experiences since my call, ordination, and setting apart. But my foundational witness of the living reality of the Father and the Son, of the great plan of happiness, and of the necessity for a latter-day restoration did not begin with nor was the product of my call to the Twelve. I have known these simple, saving truths for a long time.

Every member of this Church can and should have a testimony that qualifies him or her "to stand as [a witness] of God at all times and in all things, and in all places that ye may be in" (Mosiah 18:9). And each member has the privilege of testifying to family, friends, and associates. However, the testimony and witness of an Apostle, by virtue of the priesthood keys and authority inherent in that holy office, are different from all other officers and members of the Church (see Doctrine and Covenants 107:23).

The calling and fundamental responsibility of an Apostle is to be a special witness of the name of Jesus Christ in all the world, particularly of His divinity and of His bodily resurrection from the dead (see Acts 1:22; Doctrine and Covenants 107:23; see also Bible Dictionary, *Apostle*). Only those men called of God by prophecy to the holy apostleship receive by ordination and setting apart by the laying on of hands (1) the priesthood keys, even the ultimate authority, and (2) the ongoing responsibility to bear definitive witness of the name of Christ in all the world. These ordained special witnesses testify of the totality of the Lord's saving mission and ministry—of Him as the Divine Son of the Eternal Father, of His holy priesthood, of His redeeming work, and of the exalting purpose of the plan of salvation. These servants of the Lord act under the direction of the senior Apostle, the President of the Church, to authoritatively bind up the law, seal up the testimony, and prepare the Saints and people of the world for the hour of judgment which is to come (see Doctrine and Covenants 88:84; 109:46).

As the commotion in our world increases (see Doctrine and Covenants 45:26; 88:91), as confusion and cynicism abound concerning the nature of God and His plan for His children, as evil is called good and good is called evil (see 2 Nephi 15:20), and as "every man walketh in his own way, and after the image of his own God, whose image is in the likeness of the world, and whose substance is that of an idol" (Doctrine and Covenants 1:16), the need for apostolic authority and testimony has never been greater.

Mere mortal language cannot express adequately the sincerity and solemnity of what I yearn to communicate to you. Therefore, I pray the Holy Ghost will "fill the gap" between what I now attempt to declare with words and the earnest intent of my heart.

I witness that God the Eternal Father is our Father, even the Father of our spirits. He is the author of the great plan of happiness, and I know He is real. I witness that He lives.

Jesus Christ is the Only Begotten Son of our Heavenly Father. I witness He is divine. I also testify that He is our Redeemer and Savior. I know that the Lord Jesus Christ broke the bands of death and was resurrected. Because of the redemption and reconciliation with God that the Lord makes possible for all humankind, we can receive the spiritual assurance that "in Christ shall all be made alive" (1 Corinthians 15:22). I witness that He lives. His infinite and eternal atoning sacrifice makes possible both immortality and eternal life for each of us. I witness that all of these things are true.

I also witness that the Father and the Son appeared to Joseph Smith in 1820, thereby initiating the ongoing Restoration of the Savior's gospel and of His Church. The heavens remain open, and God reveals His will to His servants in this present day.

I joyfully share with you this apostolic witness and pray you will faithfully build the spiritual foundation of your life upon the rock of our Redeemer—today, tomorrow, and always.

I witness and testify of these supernal and eternal truths in the sacred name of the Lord Jesus Christ, amen.

NOTES

Preface

1. *Discourses of Brigham Young*, sel. John A. Widtsoe (1954), 72.
2. In Orson F. Whitney, *Life of Heber C. Kimball: An Apostle, the Father and Founder of the British Mission* (1945), 449; emphasis added.
3. In Orson F. Whitney, *Life of Heber C. Kimball*, 450; emphasis added.
4. *Teachings of Presidents of the Church: Joseph Smith* (2011), 186.
5. *Teachings of Presidents of the Church: Joseph Smith* (2011), 514–15.
6. Gordon B. Hinckley, "The Stone Cut Out of the Mountain," *Ensign*, November 2007.
7. Russell M. Nelson, "Revelation for the Church, Revelation for Our Lives," *Ensign*, May 2018.

Introduction: Building upon the Rock of Our Redeemer

1. Russell M. Nelson, "How Firm Our Foundation," *Ensign*, May 2002.
2. See also Neal A. Maxwell, "Overcome . . . Even as I Overcame," *Ensign*, May 1987.
3. *Oxford English Dictionary Online*, 2nd ed. (1989), "Steadfast."
4. *Oxford English Dictionary Online*, "Immovable."

5. Russell M. Nelson, "The Temple and Your Spiritual Foundation," *Liahona*, November 2021; emphasis in original.

6. Gary E. Stevenson, "A Good Foundation against the Time to Come," *Ensign*, May 2020.

7. Julie B. Beck, "Choose Ye This Day to Serve the Lord" (Brigham Young University Women's Conference, April 29, 2010), 4, womensconference .byu.edu.

8. Dieter F. Uchtdorf, "Missionary Work: Sharing What Is in Your Heart," *Ensign* or *Liahona*, May 2019.

Chapter 1: Bound to the Savior through Covenants

1. See *Guide to the Scriptures*, "Covenant," scriptures.ChurchofJesusChrist .org.

2. See *Guide to the Scriptures*, "Ordinances," scriptures.ChurchofJesus Christ.org.

3. Russell M. Nelson, "As We Go Forward Together," *Liahona* and *Ensign*, April 2018.

4. Dale G. Renlund, "Accessing God's Power through Covenants," *Liahona*, May 2023.

5. Russell M. Nelson, "The Everlasting Covenant," *Liahona*, October 2022.

6. Jeffrey R. Holland, "Abide in Me," *Ensign* or *Liahona*, May 2004.

7. Russell M. Nelson, "The Temple and Your Spiritual Foundation," *Liahona*, November 2021.

Chapter 2: The Blessings of Direction and Strength

1. Russell M. Nelson, "Joy and Spiritual Survival," *Liahona* and *Ensign*, November 2016.

2. Brigham Young, in *Saints: The Story of the Church of Jesus Christ in the Latter Days*, vol. 2, *No Unhallowed Hand, 1846–1893* (2020), 43. Original source: Brigham Young "to the High Council at Council

Point," September 27, 1846, Brigham Young Office Files, Church History Library, Salt Lake City.

3. *Saints*, vol. 2, *No Unhallowed Hand*, 43.

4. M. Russell Ballard, "Like a Flame Unquenchable," *Ensign*, May 1999.

Chapter 3: Armed with the Power of God in Great Glory

1. D. Todd Christofferson, "The Power of Covenants," *Ensign*, May 2009.

2. Russell M. Nelson, "Overcome the World and Find Rest," *Liahona*, November 2022.

Chapter 5: The Capacity to "Heed Not"

1. "Let Us All Press On," *Hymns*, no. 243; emphasis added.

2. "Let Us All Press On," *Hymns*, no. 243.

3. "Let Us All Press On," *Hymns*, no. 243.

4. "Let Us All Press On," *Hymns*, no. 243.

5. Joseph Smith Translation, John 1:1 reads: "In the beginning was the gospel preached through the Son. And the gospel was the word, and the word was with the Son, and the Son was with God, and the Son was of God" (in the Bible appendix).

6. "The Word" is a title of Jesus Christ found in several places in the scriptures (see John 1:1, 14; 1 John 1:1; Revelation 19:13; Doctrine and Covenants 93:8–10; Moses 1:32).

7. "Let Us All Press On," *Hymns*, no. 243.

Chapter 6: Learning for Ourselves

1. Heber C. Kimball, in "History, 1836–1844 [Manuscript History of the Church], volume E–1," 1996–97, The Joseph Smith Papers, josephsmithpapers.org.

2. Hyrum Smith, in "History, 1836–1944 [Manuscript History of the Church, volume E–1," 1994, The Joseph Smith Papers, josephsmithpapers.org.

3. Russell M. Nelson, "How Firm Our Foundation," *Ensign,* May 2002.

4. Orson F. Whitney, *Life of Heber C. Kimball* (Salt Lake City: Bookcraft, 1945), 449–50.

5. I explained this principle in a devotional in 2017:

"Alma . . . 'began to preach *the word of God* unto the people, entering into their synagogues, and into their houses; yea, and even they did preach *the word* in their streets' [Alma 32:1; emphasis added]. He also compared the word of God to a seed.

"'Now, if ye give place, that a seed may be planted in your heart, behold, if it be a true seed, or a good seed, if ye do not cast it out by your unbelief, that ye will resist the Spirit of the Lord, behold, it will begin to swell within your breasts; and when you feel these swelling motions, ye will begin to say within yourselves—It must needs be that this is a good seed, or that *the word* is good, for it beginneth to enlarge my soul; yea, it beginneth to enlighten my understanding, yea, it beginneth to be delicious to me' [Alma 32:28; emphasis added].

"Interestingly, a good seed becomes a tree as it is planted in the heart and begins to swell, sprout, and grow.

"'And behold, as *the tree* beginneth to grow, ye will say: Let us nourish it with great care, that it may get root, that it may grow up, and *bring forth fruit* unto us. And now behold, if ye nourish it with much care it will get root, and grow up, and bring forth fruit.

"'But if ye neglect the tree, and take no thought for its nourishment, behold it will not get any root; and when the heat of the sun cometh and scorcheth it, because it hath no root it withers away, and ye pluck it up and cast it out.

"'Now, this is not because the seed was not good, neither is it because the fruit thereof would not be desirable; but it is because your ground is barren, and ye will not nourish the tree, therefore ye cannot have the fruit thereof.

"'And thus, if ye will not *nourish the word,* looking forward with an eye of faith to the fruit thereof, ye can never pluck of the fruit of the tree of life.

"'But if ye will *nourish the word*, yea, *nourish the tree* as it beginneth to grow, by your faith with great diligence, and with patience, looking forward to *the fruit thereof*, it shall take root; and behold it shall be *a tree springing up unto everlasting life*' [Alma 32:37–41; emphasis added].

". . . The central feature in Lehi's dream is the tree of life—a representation of 'the love of God' [1 Nephi 11:21–22].

"'For God so loved the world, that he gave his only begotten Son, that whosoever believeth in him should not perish, but have everlasting life' [John 3:16].

"The birth, life, and atoning sacrifice of the Lord Jesus Christ are the greatest manifestations of God's love for His children. As Nephi testified, this love was 'most desirable above all things' and 'most joyous to the soul' [1 Nephi 11:22–23; see also 1 Nephi 8:12, 15]. Chapter 11 of 1 Nephi presents a detailed description of the tree of life as a symbol for the life, ministry, and sacrifice of the Savior—the 'condescension of God' [1 Nephi 11:16]. The tree can be considered as a representation of Christ.

"One way of thinking about the fruit on the tree is as a symbol for the blessings of the Savior's Atonement. The fruit is described as 'desirable to make one happy' [1 Nephi 8:10] and produces great joy and the desire to share that joy with others.

"Significantly, the overarching theme of the Book of Mormon, inviting all to come unto Christ [see Moroni 10:32], is paramount in Lehi's vision [see 1 Nephi 8:19]" ("The Power of His Word Which Is in Us" [address given at seminar for new mission leaders, June 27, 2017], 4–5).

6. Alma's analogy teaches us that the desire to believe plants the seed in our hearts, nourishing the seed by our faith sprouts the tree of life, and nourishing the tree produces fruit of the tree, which is "sweet above all that is sweet" (Alma 32:42) and is "the greatest of all the gifts of God" (1 Nephi 15:36).

Chapter 7: Line upon Line and Precept upon Precept

1. Joseph F. Smith, *Gospel Doctrine*, 5th ed. (1939), 122.
2. Neal A. Maxwell, *Wherefore Ye Must Press Forward* (Salt Lake City: Deseret Book, 1977), 73–74.
3. Spencer W. Kimball, *Faith Precedes the Miracle* (Salt Lake City: Deseret Book, 1972), 255–56.

Chapter 8: The Scriptures: A Reservoir of Living Water

1. *Teachings of the Prophet Joseph Smith,* sel. Joseph Fielding Smith (1976), 11–12.

Chapter 9: Doers of the Word

1. Joseph Smith, in "Appendix 1: First Theological Lecture on Faith, circa January–May 1835," 1, The Joseph Smith Papers, josephsmithpapers .org.
2. See David A. Bednar, "Abide in Me, and I in You; Therefore Walk with Me," *Liahona*, May 2023.
3. Joseph Smith, in "Appendix 1: First Theological Lecture on Faith, circa January–May 1835," 1, The Joseph Smith Papers, josephsmithpapers .org.
4. Russell M. Nelson, "Embrace the Future with Faith," *Ensign*, November 2020.
5. For a more thorough discussion on knowledge, understanding, and intelligence, see David A. Bednar, *Increase in Learning* (Salt Lake City: Deseret Book, 2011), 63–76.

Chapter 10: Segmenting versus Linking

1. See Spencer W. Kimball, "The Fruit of Our Welfare Services Labors," *Ensign*, November 1978.
2. "Church Consolidates Meeting Schedules," *Ensign*, March 1980.
3. "Church Consolidates Meeting Schedules," *Ensign*, March 1980.

4. See "The Family: A Proclamation to the World," *Ensign* or *Liahona*, May 2017.

5. See Gordon B. Hinckley, "New Temples to Provide 'Crowning Blessings' of the Gospel," *Ensign*, May 1998.

6. See Gordon B. Hinckley, "The Perpetual Education Fund," *Ensign*, May 2001; *Liahona*, July 2001.

7. See Russell M. Nelson, "The Sabbath Is a Delight," *Ensign* or *Liahona*, May 2015.

8. *Handbook 2: Administering the Church* (2010), 1.4; emphasis added.

Chapter 11: A More Complete and Correct Understanding

1. "When I Am Baptized," *Children's Songbook*, 103.

2. Bible Dictionary, "Baptism."

3. *Teachings of Presidents of the Church: Joseph Smith* (2011), 91.

4. Bible Dictionary, "Baptism."

5. *Teachings of Presidents of the Church: Joseph Smith*, 95–96.

6. *Teachings of Presidents of the Church: Joseph Smith*, 95.

7. *Teachings of Presidents of the Church: Joseph Smith*, 90.

Conclusion: Come unto Christ and Fear Not

1. Russell M. Nelson, "Embrace the Future with Faith," *Ensign*, November 2020; emphasis in original.

2. Neil L. Andersen, "Spiritual Whirlwinds," *Ensign*, May 2014.

3. Russell M. Nelson, "The Temple and Your Spiritual Foundation," *Liahona*, November 2021; emphasis in original.

.

INDEX

59–60; significance of, 110;
changing and turning, 112–16
Heavenly power, 37–41
Heeding not evil influences,
48–52
Helm, gospel principles and
metaphor of, 96–97
Hesed, 27
Hinckley, Gordon B., x, 92
Holland, Jeffrey R., 27–28
Holy Ghost: witness of, 16, 127–
29; power of godliness through,
38; and enlightenment
through repetition, 56–57;
spiritual knowledge through,
58–59; and ignoring worldly
influences, 58; and heart
applied to understanding, 60;
opening heart to, 81; baptism
of fire and, 91–92, 102;
receiving gift of, 92, 100–101;
link between baptism and
receiving, 101–4

Immovable, 5, 64–66
Intelligence, through obedience,
84–86. *See also* knowledge
Iron rod, 50–52, 76–77

Jesus Christ: as rock, 1–2, 7;
building spiritual foundation
on, 2–4, 117–20; faith in,
4–12, 49, 81–84, 90–91,

124–25; and covenant promises
and blessings, 14–15; binding
to, through covenants, 23–29,
43, 117; coming unto, 25–26,
117–26; abiding in, 27–29; as
source of all joy, 30; succor of,
46–47; as Word, 51; trust in,
91; as source of enduring peace,
121–22; looking to, 123–24;
apostolic witness of, 127–31.
See also Atonement; gathering
all things in Christ
Joy, 30

Kimball, Heber C., viii–ix, 56, 59
Kimball, Spencer W., 67–68, 92
Knocking, 15–17
Knowledge: acquiring, 15–17,
55–62, 63–68; and intelligence,
85–86

Latter days, ix–xi
Lehi's vision, 48–49, 76–79
"Let Us All Press On," 48, 49
Liahona, 31–32
Living water, 69–79

Malachi, 113
Marriage, 11
Maxwell, Neal A., 66–67
Mind, firmness of, 9
Missionary work, 106–16
Monson, Thomas S., 92